Zeebrugge: Learning from Disaster

Zeebrugge: Learning from Disaster

Lessons in Corporate Responsibility

Stuart Crainer

Herald Families Association

ISBN 0 9519995 0 8

Designed by Peter Dolton

Design, editorial and production in association with
Book Production Consultants,
47 Norfolk Street, Cambridge CB1 2LE

Typeset by Keystar, St Ives, Cambridge
Printed and bound by Bookcraft (Bath) Ltd, Midsomer Norton, Avon

Front cover photograph by Richard Mildenhall/*The Observer*

'We make guilty of our disasters the sun, the moon and the stars,
as if we were villains by necessity, knaves,
thieves and treachers by spherical predominance,
drunkards, liars and adulterers by an enforced
obedience of planetary influence.'

King Lear, Act 1 Scene 2

CONTENTS

6 March 1987: P&O-owned
car ferry *Herald of Free Enterprise* capsizes
off Zeebrugge; 192 passengers and crew die.

CONTENTS

PREFACE

'This was an appalling tragedy. However the recent Court decision confirms the view that there was never a case for corporate manslaughter. Let us put it behind us,' wrote Graeme Dunlop, managing director of P&O European Ferries, in Staff Newsletter No. 5 on 6 November 1990.

He was commenting on the outcome of a historic criminal trial which not only stirred up a long-overdue debate in legal circles but holds many lessons for forward-looking business executives and public servants. The trial collapsed when Mr Justice Turner directed the jury to acquit the company and seven individuals, including former directors and crew members, of the charges against them. Only a third of the evidence collected by the police had been heard. Much of the legal argument had been conducted in camera. In those circumstances the first part of Dunlop's statement may seem justified: there was insufficient evidence, a judge decided, to convict P&O European Ferries of corporate manslaughter, a charge which its counsel had strenuously (though unsuccessfully) argued did not exist in English law. The second part of the statement is, however, a disturbing reflection of the narrow thinking and reluctance to learn which lie at the heart of all easily prevented disasters.

The capsize of the *Herald of Free Enterprise* and its aftermath provide a classic case-history from which much can be learnt by people in different areas of society. That is why the Herald Charitable Trust has commissioned this book. The lessons of Zeebrugge are not restricted to the operators of shipping and other passenger services. These, of course, are industries in which directors and managers are clearly expected to do everything in their power to foresee and prevent breakdowns in operating systems. Today, however, almost every company's operations, products and services have an impact on public safety. There are disasters waiting to happen in energy, medicine, pharmaceuticals, food distribution and many other industries. Even a natural product such as water can injure or kill people if the procedures governing its distribution are poorly designed and managed.

Disaster after disaster has revealed the same pattern of incompetence, lack of foresight and irresponsibility. Safety systems and procedures have not been updated to cover changes in technology and operating conditions. The employees who implement them have not been adequately trained. Communications between top management (where the safety 'buck' starts as well as stops) and front-line employees have been poor. Directors find they can defend themselves against legal action by claiming that this or that was 'not my job' – even when they had clearly failed in their responsibility to make it *someone*'s job – or that no one had told them what was going on. All of those elements of management weakness are well documented in the case of the Zeebrugge disaster. They are also evident in other man-made disasters before and since.

There is a tendency to blame the legal system for failing to deter companies from putting profits before safety, or from tolerating sloppy management in situations which unarguably call for the highest standards of care. However, the ineffectiveness of English law in dealing with corporate crimes of violence shows up basic flaws in the governance of both companies and regulatory bodies.

The underlying theme of this book is that the most important lesson to be learnt from Zeebrugge and other disasters is that many organisations lack the leadership, structure and environment that encourage people to learn from mistakes. Changes in management attitudes would not only help to prevent disasters like Zeebrugge but would reduce the number of individual deaths or injuries caused each year by either negligent or reckless corporate behaviour.

This book draws on public documents, on the experiences of members of the Herald Families Association and on material assembled during a corporate responsibility study generously funded by The Joseph Rowntree Charitable Trust. It includes a wealth of information which was deemed either inadmissible or irrelevant at the criminal trial. It also raises questions about the role of government and the interaction between business and government.

The book jacket lists the names of 192 people, mostly young, who perished when the *Herald of Free Enterprise* suddenly rolled over on to its side in calm water. This is their book. To put them 'behind us' would be quite wrong, and would add to the terrible waste which occurred on the night of 6 March 1987. We remember them for private reasons. We wish others to understand why they were found by a coroner's jury at Dover to have been unlawfully killed and to find ways of preventing similar disasters in future.

Herald Charitable Trust

ABBREVIATIONS

The abbreviations listed here are used in this book after the first appearance of the full form.

BMT   British Maritime Technology
CPS   Crown Prosecution Service
DTI   Department of Trade and Industry
GCBS   General Council of British Shipping
HSE   Health and Safety Executive
ICAO   International Civil Aviation Organisation
IMO   International Maritime Organisation
MAIB   Marine Accident Investigation Branch
MMC   Monopolies and Mergers Commission
NUS   National Union of Seamen
PA   Press Association
RINA   Royal Institution of Naval Architects
ro-ro   roll-on, roll-off ferry

NOTE ON NAMES

The changes in titles that occurred during the period under review may be confusing to readers. The main changes sprang from P&O's decision to expunge the images of the disaster a few weeks after publication of the report of the investigation conducted by Mr Justice Sheen, Wreck Commissioner.

Townsend Thoresen's name vanished, to be replaced in the cross-Channel operation by P&O European Ferries. The livery of the vessels was changed, as were their names, with the elimination of the words 'Free Enterprise' which had acquired a horrifying connotation.

In this account the original name is used when dealing with events up to the capsize, and the present name for events after that. It was as P&O European Ferries (Dover) Ltd that the company faced the corporate manslaughter charge which was heard at the end of 1990.

SOURCES

The following reports are referred to in the text. Other references appear at the end of each chapter.

Fennell report: Department of Transport, *Investigation into the King's Cross Underground Fire*, Cm 499, HMSO, 1988.

Hidden report: Department of Transport, *Investigation into Clapham Junction Railway Accident*, Cm 820, HMSO, 1989.

MacGregor-Navire report: *Costs Associated with the Fitting of Bulkhead Doors to Existing Passenger Ro-Ro Ferries*, Report prepared for Granada Television by MacGregor-Navire Consultants, 1988.

Mersey report: *Board of Trade Inquiry under Lord Mersey*, July 1912.

Sheen report: *The Merchant Shipping Act 1984. MV Herald of Free Enterprise*, Report of Court No. 8074, HMSO, 1987.

Formal Investigation into the Collision Between the Motor Vessel European Gateway and the Motor Vessel Speedlink Vanguard, HMSO, 1984.

INTRODUCTION

Even on the verge of the twenty-first century, the world of business and commerce is fraught with dangers. Tragic disasters cloud our recent history – Aberfan, Summerland, Bradford, Zeebrugge, King's Cross, *Piper Alpha*, Hillsborough, the *Marchioness*. Virtually every business activity, if it is carried out irresponsibly, carries a grave risk – whether it be operating a nuclear power plant, mining, extracting oil from the North Sea, transporting people across the English Channel or running a football stadium.

Too often, when things go wrong scapegoats are found. Reporters and photographers sit on their doorsteps, all too willing to pile the blame on individual shoulders. Sometimes a tragedy can, in the first instance, be attributed to a single person. It may even be attributed to an act of God, though, as James Tye – director-general of the British Safety Council – has said: 'It is no use putting accidents down to acts of God. Why does God always pick on badly managed places with sloppy practices? He does not seem to pick on well managed places.'[1]

The usual background to disaster is, as history has repeatedly shown, a compendium of error and misjudgement – not only by individuals, but groups, boards and companies. Though the act or omission of an individual may precipitate disaster, the real cause lies much deeper within the systems, outlook and personnel of an organisation.

At Chernobyl in 1986, investigations revealed 'deliberate, systematic and numerous violations' of safety procedures. At King's Cross in 1987, the Fennell report found senior management to have had 'narrow horizons, blinkered self-sufficiency'. On the North Sea oil rig *Piper Alpha*, fire-fighting equipment was 'virtually useless' and had been so for four months – 167 people died. After the rail crash at Clapham Junction in

1

1988 the official inquiry found 'bad workmanship, poor supervision and poor management'. British Rail was eventually fined £250,000 after admitting failing to ensure that its employees and passengers were not exposed to risk.

The aim of this book is to focus on one particular disaster and learn lessons from it which are applicable to all managers and companies, no matter what their business is.

All managers face crises. How they handle these when they do arise and how they create systems to avoid them arising are vital aspects of their professional expertise. A cunningly conceived corporate strategy is worthless if it endangers life. Irresponsible thinking or inadequate monitoring leads to irresponsible and dangerous practice.

The company: untouched and untouchable?

A common thread running through Zeebrugge and other tragedies is that management could, and should, have played a central part in preventing them. Management could have engendered attitudes of mind and systems which would have created responsible and safe working practices. The capsize of the ro-ro car ferry *Herald of Free Enterprise* off Zeebrugge in March 1987 cost many lives. Scapegoats were found. It was, however, primarily a disaster of management.

In the immediate aftermath, blame was attached to the ship's assistant bosun, who failed to close its bow doors, the primary cause of the disaster. The captain and first officer were also criticised. With the public inquiry, under Mr Justice Sheen, attention shifted to the behaviour of management and the corporate responsibility of P&O, the ship's owner, for the disaster. It had only recently taken over European Ferries and its subsidiary Townsend Thoresen, whose name was emblazoned on the ship's sides. Under Townsend's management, warnings and suggestions from captains had been ignored or frivolously rejected. Procedures on board ship were vaguely worded, and on the Zeebrugge run required one officer to be in two places at once. Some of the shore managers were unsure of what their jobs actually entailed and sometimes had little or no seafaring experience. They put captains and crews under pressure to operate as speedily as possible.

'Cardinal faults lay higher up in the company,' said the Sheen report. 'From top to bottom, the body corporate was infected with the disease of sloppiness.' This startling condemnation was shortly followed by verdicts of unlawful killing at the coroner's court.

Over three years after the disaster, members of the crew and former directors of Townsend Thoresen were charged with manslaughter, along with the company itself, by then renamed P&O European Ferries. With the charging of P&O, the ramifications of the case became even wider. It was only the second time in British legal history that a company had been charged with manslaughter. The decision to prosecute in itself seemed to mark an important step forward in the development of the principle of corporate accountability. But after 27 days in the Central Criminal Court, the judge directed the jury to acquit the defendants on all charges. In his eyes, the prosecution case was unsustainable.

The events in court left many people, not only those directly affected by the disaster, wondering whether justice had indeed been done. There appeared to be a widening gulf between the public's perception of justice and the legalistic interpretation of it. The prosecution counsel was up against an array of the country's most experienced and expensive barristers. Outnumbered and outclassed, the prosecution never got off the ground. Much of the trial was carried out in the absence of the jury and seemed bogged down in legal technicalities rather than concerning itself with the deaths of innocent people. Issues such as the governance of companies and the responsibilities of directors and senior managers were all but ignored.

While hundreds of people had their lives tragically transformed by the Zeebrugge disaster, the company to all intents and purposes remained untouched and untouchable. Within months, the name Townsend Thoresen ceased to exist. The company became P&O European Ferries.

The tragic case of the *Herald* brought to light many critical issues facing managers and businesses in the 1990s and beyond:

* It confronted the entire idea of balancing profits against safety and was even seen by some as an indictment of the free enterprise system.
* It demonstrated the need for expert input, constant monitoring and the ability to listen to professionals in order to reach the highest standards in the design of products and services.
* It showed, once and for all, that safety has to be a board level responsibility and that simply conforming to regulations is not enough to protect customers and employees adequately.
* It made clear the need for managers to understand and deal with the

concerns of employees, demonstrating that human relationships are not about extracting every available minute of work from tired employees but about increasing the quality of work and job satisfaction.

* It exposed the dangers of poor communications systems. Well-grounded fears expressed by employees and senior masters were ignored. So was positive criticism of the company's operations.

* Crucially, the Zeebrugge disaster brought to greater prominence the question of where management's responsibilities lie. Despite the protestations of senior managers that they were not ultimately responsible, the responsibility of managers for the day-to-day activities of their organisation is now being closely examined.

* The fact that P&O had only recently acquired Townsend highlighted the responsibilities of companies (and those who advise them) in takeovers. It also provoked debate about what companies should look at beyond the balance sheet when making an acquisition.

* The relationship between P&O and the government brought to the surface important questions about what kind of links major corporations and their senior managers should have with related government departments.

This catalogue of important issues shows that the net of responsibility is much wider than has been generally recognised. Though scapegoats are still found, people realise that in the modern corporation no man is an island. Companies have responsibilities not only for their own employees and users of their products, but for members of the communities in which they operate. Directors and senior managers cannot be allowed to remain loftily detached from the day-to-day activities of their companies. They are not strategists ensconced in ivory towers but the people who shape the way employees carry out their duties.

Zeebrugge showed that directors and managers need to have a much clearer idea of what their jobs entail. While those lower down the corporate hierarchy have their duties and jobs strictly defined, those at the top often carry on without such guidelines. What matters is not 'being' a company director, but acting in the way a director should. In too many cases it appears that the very vagueness of their duties enables managers to avoid facing up to direct responsibility. Yet logic and morality insist that responsibility is not solely the preserve of someone repetitively operating a machine or carrying out a relatively menial role. If an assistant bosun is accountable for his actions, so too must his superiors be.

Balance sheets are no consolation to the bereaved

The loss of the *Herald* tragically demonstrated that successful management and business should be based on accepting, implementing and developing a sense of corporate responsibility within an organisation. Corporate success is not simply a question of healthy balance sheets. They are no consolation to the bereaved and do not necessarily prove that a company is well run. This is not a sudden revelation. The growing interest in corporate responsibility, a vital aspect of management practice, is a logical progression from some of the preoccupations of management thinkers in recent years. Its roots lie in the surge of interest in business ethics in the early 1970s – though it can be said to go back as far as Robert Owen's enlightened sense of responsibility in his Scottish textile mills in the early nineteenth century.

Many companies in the 1970s produced codes of practice for both managers and employees. There were social audits to determine the impact of the company's activities on the local community and the world beyond. As with so many other management fads, interest quickly waned. The noble aspirations and public relations statements did not lead to significant action. The twenty years since then have seen management theory change dramatically. More than ever before managers are encouraged to look outside the narrow confines of their office and what they believe their job to be. They are told to get out and see for themselves what is going on within their organisation, to take a look at the results of their strategies rather than regarding strategy as a self-fulfilling prophecy. They have looked abroad to learn lessons from Japan and have sought to adopt the best through the 'excellence' movement.

Business misconduct can damage
and destroy lives

The horizons of managers have had to expand. The great challenges they now face are no longer local. They are not only economic but international, environmental and ethical. To some extent, managers are driven by fear. There is fear that if they don't put their own house in order someone else will, whether it be the European Community, the government or another regulatory body. They have seen corporate irresponsibility and unethical behaviour identified and punished. 'There are few ways in which a man can be more innocently employed than in getting money,' quipped Dr Johnson in 1775. Two hundred years later, such innocence is hard won and can no longer be assumed. The Guinness scandal, for example, saw three respected businessmen jailed for conspiracy, fraud and theft on a mammoth scale. Companies which have polluted the environment have been punished.

The dramatic rise in man-made disasters, all of them preventable, has made the subject all the more pressing. These catastrophes have shown that even companies with carefully worded codes of practice can act irresponsibly at times. They have also made managers and the public aware that business misconduct is not restricted to technical offences such as insider-dealing or share-pushing, but can damage and destroy the lives of ordinary people. The behaviour of companies has not necessarily worsened. But it has, in many cases, failed to keep pace with fundamental changes in technology, the market-place, consumer behaviour and social expectations.

The rapid pace of technological change means that simply keeping abreast of developments is time consuming and, in some businesses, beyond the scope of many managers. Airline pilots, for example, are among the best trained and most highly skilled professionals. Yet recent evidence suggests that they are liable to be overwhelmed by the changing technological content of their job. In 1989 a British Midland plane crashed on the M1 motorway when the crew shut down the wrong engine. They had misread instruments. An Air India plane crashed when the computer overrode the pilot's commands. The work of a pilot was once manual and mechanical. Today it is increasingly mental. A pilot needs to understand what his computer is doing before he can understand what the plane itself is doing. The same is true of managers in earthbound occupations.

Companies will increasingly be unable
to hide behind human error

There tends to be an assumption that technological progress makes things safer and more reliable. This is not necessarily true. The *Herald of Free*

Enterprise was a 7-year-old ship which met all the safety standards then in operation. It capsized in a fraction of the time a traditional passenger vessel is expected to stay afloat in an emergency to allow for the evacuation of passengers. In this, and many other instances, progress had failed to enhance performance and safety.

While technology has been revolutionising the way work is done, a less obvious revolution has been occurring in consumer behaviour and social expectations. The 1980s brought new notions of customer service and quality. These are now being supplemented by the concerns of the consumer about the environment and about the way products are made and the working conditions of those who make them. Consumers continually attest to their willingness to pay more for ethically, environmentally or even politically 'acceptable' products, whether they be soap powder or a new car. Companies such as Body Shop have succeeded because of their ethical and responsible approach, not in spite of it. What started as a marketing man's dream is rapidly becoming one of the foremost principles of business.

Such changes are strikingly evident in the air transport industry. Technology enables us to travel faster than ever before to virtually anywhere on the globe. The market-place is fiercely competitive and our expectations are high. We expect to travel safely, in comfort and at an affordable price. The demand for a higher level of corporate responsibility is clear and the operators, in general, have responded to it well. In other branches of passenger transportation, the picture is less encouraging. Customers assume, sometimes mistakenly, that such companies automatically accept the mantle of responsibility. Though they usually travel comfortably and safely enough, the issue of who takes responsibility when things go wrong is complex. On a bus, for example, is it the driver or the bus company, or a combination of both? On an aircraft, is it the pilot or the airline? On a cross-Channel ferry, is it the captain or shore management?

The extraordinary capsize of the *Herald of Free Enterprise* made it quite clear that responsibility stretches far beyond the confines of the ship. It reaches the managers who establish procedures and working conditions; the directors who set the strategy and direction of the company; the financiers who put together takeover deals; the politicians who legislate and respond to lobbying; the designers who create the product in the first place.

*The organisation with no sense of
responsibility will have no place in the
business world of tomorrow*

The Zeebrugge manslaughter case reached a legal dead end. But it has ensured that corporate responsibility has become an important issue for all involved in management. It has also brought the matter of 'corporate manslaughter' on to the legal agenda. These substantial steps forward mean that companies will increasingly be unable to hide behind human error. Managers will have to stand by their decisions and form strategies and practices which achieve higher standards and not necessarily lower costs. They will not be able to claim immunity from charges of negligence or recklessness on the ground that they did not know what was happening. They will have to accept that it is their job to find out, not to wait to be told.

As the corporate responsibility issue becomes more widely understood, consumers will become more selective. No longer will they automatically obey the first principles of economics described in Adam Smith's *Wealth of Nations*. 'In every country it always is and must be the interest of the great body of people to buy whatever they want of those who sell it cheapest. The proposition is so very manifest that it seems ridiculous to take any pains to prove it,' wrote Smith over two hundred years ago. Today, he would face quite a challenge to prove what was once deemed to be self-explanatory.

Changes in the facts of commercial life are already taking place. Brands, for example, are becoming more closely identified with a company's stance and record on pollution, health and safety and the use of natural resources. In future, more and more people will choose not to work for or buy from the cavalier company intent on short-term results, no matter what the cost. The organisation with no sense of its social and moral responsibility will have no place in the business world of tomorrow. Companies must act, and be seen to act, in a responsible way to employees, customers and the environment. Those that fail to do so will simply fail. The end-result will be more responsible management and companies which offer increased safety, better quality and greater customer satisfaction. Through those achievements they will gain higher profits.

References

1. Quoted in 'The Consumer, the Lawyer and the Company', Rodger Pannone, paper presented at Consumer Congress 16th Annual Conference, Belfast, 6 April 1991.

CHAPTER ONE

DISASTER

'She wobbled a bit, then went over'
– assistant purser on the *Herald*.

'I knew the doors were open. My first thought was the doors.'
– assistant bosun on the *Herald*.

For the crew of the Townsend Thoresen ferry, *Herald of Free Enterprise*, 6 March 1987 was a day as normal as any other. The weather was fine and dry, but cold. The ship had crossed from Dover at 11.30 and was due to leave the Belgian port of Zeebrugge at 18.00. It was a journey it and its sister ships had safely completed many thousands of times before. On arrival in port, the great bow doors of the ship were opened by assistant bosun Mark Stanley. As the cars and lorries left the ferry he carried out some maintenance and cleaning. His work completed, Stanley was dismissed by the bosun, Terry Ayling.

Each crew was on board ship for 24 hours and then had 48 hours on shore. These long hours meant that it was common for crew members to sleep or relax for parts of their time on board. Stanley had been working since 10.30. He returned to his cabin and fell asleep. As Stanley slept, the call of 'harbour stations' was announced over the ship's public address system. The crew took up their positions for departure from Zeebrugge's no. 12 berth.

First officer Leslie Sabel was on the car deck, now filled with 81 cars, three buses and 47 lorries. Looking around as the ship prepared for departure, he thought he saw Stanley heading towards the panel of controls which closed the bow doors. Sabel, believing things were progressing normally, climbed up to the bridge to his post for departure. As he did so, the ship – 433 feet long and weighing 7,950 gross tons – reversed out of the dock. Its passengers began to disperse into its bars and duty-free shops. Many of them had been on a cheap day trip to Belgium offered in a *Sun* newspaper promotion.

The ship swung round, its bow doors still open but out of sight of the captain and the other officers on the bridge. At 18.20 it passed the inner harbour breakwater and began to accelerate towards the open sea. When its speed was between 15 and 18 knots, water began to enter the car deck through the open doors. Because not all of the water had been pumped out of the ship's bow ballast tanks, the bow of the *Herald of Free Enterprise* was two or three feet lower in the water than normal. Water entered the car deck at a rate of 200 tons every minute. Almost instantly the *Herald* listed 30 degrees to port. The water continued to flood in. At 18.25, exactly 23 minutes after its departure, the ferry turned right round and rolled over on to a sandbank less than a mile from the harbour. Only its starboard half remained above the water. The rest of this huge ship was submerged, leaving its 80 crew and 459 panic-stricken passengers to fight for their lives.

The speed of the disaster gave no time for preparation. There was no chance of grabbing a lifebelt or finding where the lifeboats were. There was no warning, no announcement. The ship's lighting flickered and then went out. Emergency lighting failed. Within seconds the vessel was on its side, half of it under water.

Second officer Paul Morter was having a meal break. Examining the menu, he 'heard a dull thud and a slight tremor'. He recalled:

> Then I realised the ship was heeling over to port as if turning to starboard. I realised something abnormal was happening and I dashed for the bridge. I saw the master by the ship's console. By this time I had to hang on to stop myself sliding to port. I recall seeing the chief officer falling from starboard to port as the heel increased. The port bridge was going into the water. I recall hearing alarm bells and hearing the master give the orders to close the bow watertight doors.

But it was too late. 'Water was coming up the bridge front window. Water was pouring into the bridge,' said Morter. He fell into the water, surfacing near the ship's steering console. He heard Ostend radio calling the ship repeatedly.

She wobbled a bit, then went over

The first time Stephen Homewood, the ship's assistant purser, heard anything unusual was when he took a message from John Butler, a steward. Butler said there was water pouring down the stairs on E deck below the car deck. He believed it was a burst pipe. 'Within seconds of the call the ship began to list. She wobbled a bit, then went over,' said Homewood.

> The furniture started to move. The bar was busy with people. I remember all the people on the starboard side flying through the air and hitting glass windows on the port side. There was no time to phone the bridge. Water began to come through the glass and then the lights failed. The emergency lights came on for a few seconds and then went out. Paul [White – the ship's cook] was nearest the door; he got out first and pulled me out.

Homewood then began to lift people through a door overhead and to pass lifejackets out to passengers in the water.

> A diver went down in the water where a lot of lifejackets were floating. I tied people to the rope but some gave up and slipped back. Glenn Butler was there. He said he was all right. Later, when a diver reached him, he was dead.
>
> There was a diver in the water working tremendously hard, but needing assistance, especially in saving people's lives as there were people there without lifejackets and they were still alive. Some were hanging on to ropes. There was an accumulation of dead bodies at the base of the ladder and I am sure they were floating on top of them.

Even though he fell in the water himself, Homewood stayed on the wreck for six hours, going back to help people to safety. He was later awarded the Queen's Gallantry Medal.

Others of the crew performed similar heroics to reduce the death toll. Michael Tracy, the ship's carpenter, spent two hours on the side of the ship helping to pull passengers out. He said:

> I heard a lot of crashing noises as cars and lorries fell on the car deck. We got some axes from the lifeboats and began breaking the windows to the passenger accommodation. The assistant bosun went further aft and did the same. At this stage we found there was considerable confusion and panic among the passengers.

Bosun Terry Ayling took charge of the rescue operation, organising the crew into rescue parties. 'We shouted not to panic – she has settled and is not going further down. Some of the crew climbed down into the passenger accommodation to help others out.'

I knew the doors were open.
My first thought was the doors

Able seaman Leigh Cornelius formed the bottom of a ladder of crew members standing one on top of the other in order to enable passengers to climb to safety. Head waiter Michael Skippen tried to calm people down even when the restaurant was under several feet of water. He died at his post and was posthumously awarded the George Medal. Quartermaster Richard Hobbs stayed at the wheel of the ferry as she tilted over and as a result lost his life.

Mark Stanley also played a major part in rescuing passengers and crew. Within minutes of the accident, however, he said: 'As soon as the ship started rolling I knew the doors were open. My first thought was the doors. I thought, you know, the doors have not been shut. I knew I had not shut them ... I was just hoping that someone had shut them.'[1]

The ship's master, Captain David Lewry, insisted on staying on the ship as long as possible before being rescued by a tug. He later recalled how quickly the disaster happened.

> The ship started to turn to starboard and immediately was going over. It was that fast, I was looking in the radar and though they say it might have taken a little longer, she went over in 90 seconds.
>
> In seconds the ship was going to starboard and then she was tipping over. So much races through your mind. My immediate reaction was to stop the bloody ship and I pulled all the handles back to full-astern to do that. I knew we were in serious trouble, I said, 'Oh my God, what's going on?'
>
> I tried to get to the VHF radio but I didn't because the ship had gone over and I couldn't reach it. There were things sliding all around the wheelhouse. I was thrown 30 or 40 feet. The next thing I remember I was floating. I was still inside the wheelhouse and the big anorak I was wearing was keeping me afloat.
>
> Eventually, I was hauled out. I heard no shouts or screaming. I

had no time to even think that I might die, or that passengers and crew were dying. No time.[2]

One of the crew, Nicky Delo, said: 'I saw two figures standing on the hull. The boatswain said to me "The captain's hurt. He can't do anything, get him off". I put my arms around him, but he struggled and pulled away from me. He just did not want to leave.'

For the passengers all was darkness. But, on what had started off as an unexceptional day, ordinary people performed heroic acts to rescue passengers and crew.

It was like swimming in black ink

Andrew Parker, an assistant finance manager at a City bank, was in the ship's cafe with his family. 'My daughter flew past me and crashed into the side of the corridor,' he said. In darkness, he organised a group of passengers to climb along seats only to reach a 6-foot wide space full of water. 'I jumped down and spread myself in the water. I arched my back and held on to the railings on the other side so people could use me as a stepping stone.' Safely across, the group reached another space full of water. The only escape was 15 feet above. 'Someone outside half opened the double doors and dropped a rope through the hole.' As the rope hung, offering escape, two drunks forced their way to the front but fell into the water to perish. 'Everyone became more calm, particularly after seeing these two men fall in,' said Parker. Two hours later all of the group had climbed the rope to the precarious hull of the ship. Andrew Parker was later awarded the George Medal for what he described as an 'act of practicality rather than bravery'.

Passengers saw loved ones die in front of them. Passenger Peter Williamson saw his friend drown, unable to pull himself to safety. 'I was almost suffocated from the vapour of the duty-free bottles exploding,' he said. Another recalled, 'it was like swimming in black ink'.

Alan Rogers was in the ship's video lounge with his family.

Within seconds we were right on our side. There were people walking and caught completely unawares flying through the air. Trays, drinks, you name it, fell. We were being peppered with missiles. People who went through the glass were just torn to

14

shreds. Within seconds it went black. There was no transition. You heard the water rush and it was up around you. It was pandemonium.

On shore, reaction was swift. The nearby dredger, *Sanderus*, raised the alarm. At 7.10pm a red alert sounded at the Plymouth headquarters of the Armed Services Rescue Command. Squadron Leader Ian Challas wrote in the logbook, 'Dover coastguards have informed us that a vessel, the *Herald of Free Enterprise*, is believed to have capsized off Zeebrugge.' Helicopters, divers and paramedics were scrambled from an array of bases throughout Britain – Sea King helicopters came from RAF Brawdy in Dyfed and RAF Coltishall near Norwich, while others prepared at Culrose, Cornwall. Belgian rescue services were already at the scene. Lieutenant Steve Wild led the Royal Navy divers in the rescue. 'If the Belgian people had not used their initiative and reacted spontaneously and enthusiastically, the number of survivors would have been reduced dramatically,' he said.

There were a lot of people pulling survivors off the wreck so it was obviously a little disorganised, but the priority was speed. As soon as the accident happened, there was an appeal for help on the radio and the rescue services, merchant seamen, people with boats and members of the public rushed to the ship to get people off.

The word horrific is used too often ...
but I can use it with its full impact

An RAF pathologist later said that the waters around the ship were so cold that even highly trained swimmers would have started to sink within two minutes. The last three survivors were found at 1.15 in the morning.

After the tragedy, teams of British and Belgian divers spent a month bringing some of the dead out of the ship. The divers struggled through black evil-smelling mud, oil and debris. They told of seeing the bodies of a man and woman locked in a final embrace, a girl aged about 11 still cradling a doll, and a 'tangle' of 20 victims piled against a bulkhead. 'I think we will all suffer long-term scarring in our minds that will live with us for ever,' said Commander Jack Birkett, leader of the British team. 'The word horrific is used too often these days, but I can use it with its full impact.'

Long after the disaster, confusion reigned. On 6 April, a month afterwards, Belgian authorities claimed 61 people had died and 132 were still missing, their bodies taken by the sea or locked in the wreck of the *Herald*. Kent police agreed with this figure. The ferry company, however, insisted that only 73 people were missing. 'There were 543 on board the ferry; 409 were rescued. 61 bodies have been recovered, and 73 are missing, 33 of these crew members,' its spokesman explained. 'We had a ticket and head count at the port.'[3]

In fact, 192 people died in the *Herald of Free Enterprise* (and one survivor died later). The true figure was not accepted by Townsend Thoresen until the ship was righted and the majority of the bodies recovered. There was some speculation about the ferry company's reason for clinging to their false figures. In a letter to *The Daily Telegraph* on 10 April, the P&O chairman, Sir Jeffrey Sterling (now Lord Sterling of Plaistow), blamed the chaos of the rescue operations. He did not try to explain why the company had not amended its false estimate in the light of subsequent evidence. Most observers, meanwhile, were surprised to learn that a major shipping company did not reliably count the number of passengers boarding its vessels.

On a calm day, the capsize of a modern ferry had claimed the worst death toll for a British vessel in peace-time since the sinking of the *Titanic* in 1912. Terrifyingly, the disaster could have been a lot worse. A few minutes later, the *Herald* would have been in the open seas. It is unlikely many, if any, would have survived if the ferry had sunk a few hundred yards further into the English Channel.

References

1. *Guardian*, 20 October 1990.
2. *Daily Express*, 24 February 1988.
3. *The Daily Telegraph*, 6 April 1987.

CHAPTER TWO

THE PROFIT MOTIVE

'My first responsibility is to the
shareholders of P&O
and profit is what it is all about.'
– Jeffrey Sterling, P&O chairman.

'… the legacy of this terrible tragedy will be that
those who died paid the price of free enterprise.'
– Simon Hughes MP.

'We exist to make profits,' observed John Cahill when chief executive of
one of Britain's largest companies, BTR. In the enterprise culture of the
1980s the bottom line was all important. Blinded by the need for short-
term results, some companies could seemingly excuse any misadventure
or negligence as long as profits were sustained and increased. It was a
trend upheld by the belief that, above all else, shareholders and institutional investors are interested in financial value.

Profit is what it is all about

'British industry is seen as being too partial towards its shareholders and
top managers at the expense of investment, its workforce and its customers,' concluded the annual publication *British Social Attitudes*[1] in the year
after the Zeebrugge disaster. When asked where corporate profits went,
34 per cent of members of the public replied in increased dividends for
shareholders. When asked where profits *should* go, 29 per cent replied
they should be invested in new machinery. Only 3 per cent thought they
should lead to increased dividends.

For some highly successful business people, enhancing shareholder
value is the key aim of business. 'The central tenet of my faith is that the
shareholder is king,' says Lord Hanson.[2]

The priority given to share value and the well-being of shareholders was demonstrated in the case of the Fayed takeover of House of Fraser and its retail flagship, Harrods. The Department of Trade and Industry (DTI) examination of the takeover concluded that the Fayeds had misrepresented their wealth, business interests and resources to the Secretary of State, the Office of Fair Trading, the press, the House of Fraser board and their own advisers. But, since the interests of shareholders had not been adversely affected, no action was taken. The Fayeds remained in control of one of London's most prestigious stores. Financial value emerged the victor over troublesome ethics.

The belief in the profit motive above all else can be seen in the way senior executives explain what they are in business to do. They often develop BTR's simple – and successful – theme. 'We secure our future by achieving sustained levels of profit on the capital we invest. That is the only way,' wrote Sterling in P&O's 1987 annual report. In the same year he also commented, 'We are not in shipping. Shipping is not a business, it is a method.' P&O, he said, is in the 'transport of freight and human beings'.[3] Sterling has also emphasised his overriding duty to provide dividends for shareholders. 'My first responsibility is to the shareholders of P&O and profit is what it is all about. We will run our fleet in the most profitable way for our shareholders,' he told *Lloyd's List* in 1991.[4] The driving force behind the business, it appears, is the need to provide dividends for shareholders.

In response, Labour MP John Prescott, then shadow Transport Secretary, caustically observed that P&O is 'more interested in property returns than shipping'.[5]

Stung by such criticism, Sterling has lamented, 'Whatever I say, I am [regarded as] a captain of industry and a capitalist beggar who is only interested in making a profit.'[6] That he has other interests Sterling made clear in a speech to the Institute of Directors' 1990 conference in which he called for a longer-term approach and was critical of short-term attitudes among shareholders. He called for 'clear-headed and sensitive management', backed by shareholders acting like owners rather than mere investors. This, however, rests uneasily with his exhortations on the merits of profit.

The importance of producing a healthy return on capital employed is so obvious that it hardly needs to be stated. Yet in the post-war decades some of Britain's fine old companies seemed to have lost sight of it. That probably accounts for the uncompromising message which P&O's newly appointed chairman delivered to his managers in 1985 after fighting off a hostile (and, at first sight, irresistible) bid by Trafalgar House for the 150-year-old shipping company. 'Our financial survival and personal welfare,' Sterling warned them, 'depends upon our ability to produce a level of profit in each of our businesses that justifies our claim to the title of "manager". In the absence of that constantly improving financial result, we have no claim – historical or otherwise.'

By concentrating on the short term,
such companies ignored
some of the foundations of long-term prosperity

It was a stirring battle-cry for a company that, according to its official history,[7] had 'faced extinction'. Any business – whether it is manufacturing engineering components or transporting millions of people across the world's busiest sea lane – can be seen as a means to an end. Some companies advocating this philosophy did not survive the 1980s; it was a policy fraught with commercial danger. By concentrating on the short term, such companies ignored some of the foundations of long-term prosperity. Opportunities to invest in R&D, quality improvement, employee training and customer satisfaction sunk to the bottom of the in-tray. The fate of the companies that followed this blinkered thinking can be read about in many of the corporate obituaries in the City pages of today's newspapers.

Though attitudes are now changing, there is still a mistaken impression that profitability and high safety levels are incompatible – or, at best, a delicate balancing act. Spend too much money on safety and your company will lose ground to hard-nosed competitors! Its share price may also plummet. The truth, however, is that in the medium to long term that investment is likely to pay off by reducing down-time as well as insurance, administration, plant maintenance and other related costs.

Managements have also to consider how the unforeseen costs of a disaster would damage the balance sheet and even threaten their survival. For a major group with diverse interests and a good profits record, this would not necessarily be an insuperable problem. An estimate by the Herald Families Association put the direct cost of the *Herald*'s capsize at £80–90 million, much of it met by insurance companies. This produced barely a hiccup in P&O's 'sustained level of profit'. Even in 1988, the

19

year after the Zeebrugge disaster, the group recorded profits of £267.7 million, up by 21 per cent on the previous year. But a disaster on the same scale could easily wipe out a smaller, single-activity company – or, indeed, a major company already in financial difficulty.

Despite insurance cover, the direct costs of disasters are rising steadily while the hidden costs in image and public relations terms are rising even faster

---

British Petroleum, an acknowledged leader in safety, now justifies safety expenditure by conducting the same kind of cost–benefit analysis that it applies to all other business decisions. How much would it cost if non-implementation of a particular safety measure were to result in a disaster or major accident? This is a realistic approach. Despite insurance cover, the direct costs of disasters are rising steadily while the hidden costs in image and public relations terms are rising even faster. According to one estimate, over 60 per cent of the industrial sites where there is a serious 'incident' actually cease operating.[8] A notable example is the Union Carbide plant at Bhopal in India; the company was hard-hit by the financial and emotional aftermath of a disaster in which 2,500 people died.

The scale of financial penalties is further demonstrated by the costs incurred by Exxon after its tanker, the *Exxon Valdez*, polluted a huge stretch of the coast of Alaska. The company spent $2 billion on clearing up the damage, in addition to making payments totalling $1.1 billion to the US and Alaskan authorities.

Of course, every company in every business will say that safety is paramount and never compromised by the pursuit of profit. 'We do not do anything at all that would jeopardise safety. We are seeking the standards of excellence,' said a P&O spokesman some months after the Zeebrugge disaster.[9]

For companies in the transport business there is a catch-22. Competition is traditionally based on the ability to meet timetable demands rather than on quality of service or safety. If a company fails to compete on these terms, it simply fails to compete. Safety is not usually deemed to offer a 'competitive edge'. This is nothing new. The report of Lord Mersey into the loss of the *Titanic* concluded that its speed was excessive, but in accordance with the long-existing customs due to competition and to the desire of the public for quick passages rather than to the lack of judgement by navigators. But the high speed kept up in the icefield was due to nobody's negligence or ignorance and the track followed was reasonably safe with proper vigilance.

The passengers, it seems, were at fault for wanting to reach their destination quickly. The professionals to whom they entrusted their lives were simply obeying the wishes of the paying customers rather than paying heed to their own training and responsibility.

Competition is reaching suicidal levels

The argument put forward by ship owners (and managers in many other businesses) is that independent action on safety actually reduces competitiveness. If they invest heavily in safety and their competitors do not, those competitors will produce more impressive short-term balance sheets, their own shares will fall in value, potential investors will look elsewhere and (to close the vicious circle) there will be no money available to invest in higher safety in future. Most boards of directors want a level playing field where every company is obliged – one way or another – to spend the same amount on safety. In those circumstances there would be no economic reason for a company not to support realistic safety principles. But companies do not exist in such an ideal environment, and it is unlikely they ever will do so. Consequently, few are prepared to take the risk of prejudicing the glory of a healthy profit by investing more heavily in safety. Instead, they spend their time looking over their shoulders to see what competitors are doing. Business remains, to a large extent, a reactive occupation.

In an imperfect world, there is likely to be someone spending less money on safety than any individual company. There is never 100 per cent safety, of course, and no matter what the business, there is always a small minority of manufacturers or suppliers who are either reckless or grossly negligent. They present unfair competition to the vast majority who build proper safety standards into their operations and costings.

In the shipping industry part of the problem appears to lie in the attitude to standardised financial accounting and operating statistics. The International Civil Aviation Organisation (ICAO) has a standardised international approach, but shipping does not. It is, therefore, difficult to quantify some of the issues into their financial or economic equivalents. Cost–benefit analysis, a fundamental part of many business decisions, is given little credence in shipping circles. The International Maritime Organisation (IMO) has never commissioned any cost–benefit analysis. The Department of Transport is similarly unenthusiastic. It does not use the idea in the maritime field, but does so for other modes of transport. The lack of interest in studying the economics of shipping safety is perhaps shown by the fact that Lloyd's Register of Shipping does not employ a single economist. This general attitude merely broadens the gulf between operational safety and financial success. In the eyes of the shipping world, finance remains at the whim of the operator. With no ground rules or standards, the cost (and cost benefits) of investment in safety will never be known. As a result, managers are unable to argue that improved safety standards will bring clear and measurable financial benefits.

Lack of clarity is not the only element impinging on safety. In the cross-Channel ferry market the need to keep down costs and eliminate unnecessary expenditure is especially great, and is likely to become even greater with the opening of the Channel tunnel. Shortly after the Zeebrugge tragedy, on 10 March 1987, *The Daily Telegraph*, a newspaper not much given to hyperbole, offered an overview of the state of the cross-Channel ferry business.

> Competition is reaching suicidal levels among ferry firms, with some collapsing and all making big economies. Experienced travel- lers at Dover haggle over fares in the ferry terminal like bargain hunters in an Arab bazaar, going from counter to counter to see who will offer the biggest discount off-peak. International road hauliers demand huge discounts for laden lorries and other cargo ... the problems are worsening fast with most operators in trouble.

The newspaper attributed some of the blame to the government's decision in 1979 to break up what it called 'the unofficial cartel by which Channel companies liaised on fares and sailing'.

Unbeatable on price, speed and facilities

Competition was then at fever pitch and a number of companies had already bitten the dust or been forced into radical restructuring. British and Irish Steam Packet was in the throes of a strike after it tried to introduce a cost-cutting programme, and was making heavy losses. Others, such as Hover Lloyd and Seaspeed, had been forced to merge. P&O's London–Ostend hydrofoil route had closed and Sealink was demanding manning cuts on its services. The situation was intensified by the prospect of the Channel tunnel. Though Sealink's chairman James Sherwood launched a last-minute bid for a tunnel scheme, ferry operators were understandably wary of this threat to their business. This soon developed into bullishness as they recognised that the tunnel was unlikely to eliminate completely the need for cross-Channel ferries. In 1986, Townsend had proclaimed that it could build a fleet of ships to equal the capacity of the tunnel and at half the price.[10]

Confidence in the existing fleet was forcibly expressed by a P&O spokesman only a month after the Zeebrugge disaster: 'We have invested £85 million with the specific objective of ensuring these ships are unbeatable on price, speed and facilities'.[11] It is significant that even at this most difficult moment in the company's history his list of competitive advantages did not emphasise safety.

Back in 1986 the ferry companies had already begun to feel the cold wind of new competition. With the Channel tunnel now emerging as a reality rather than an improbable engineering feat, the need to run their operations as tightly as possible was greater than ever before. It was in this environment that the *Herald* was to make its final passenger-carrying voyage. The very name of the vessel, and of others of the same class, was a celebration of the 1980s' rediscovery of entrepreneurialism and market forces.

After the disaster, Simon Hughes of the Liberal Democrats, in the House of Commons, drew out the link between the *Herald* and the culture it represented:

> Unless action is taken, and unless the Secretary of State concedes that gross negligence occurred as a result of the behaviour of the company and possibly that of the Department, the legacy of this terrible tragedy will be that those who died paid the price of free enterprise. That will be the motto of this incident.[12]

This is political hyberbole, of course, but in view of the revelations then being made at the Sheen inquiry even those of different political persuasions were hard pressed to refute his suggestion entirely.

An important element in the capsize of the *Herald* was the company's preoccupation with keeping to time, ensuring that it outstripped or at least matched its rivals in that respect. This was a long-standing concern. Improvements in the design of roll-on, roll-off ferries (ro-ros) had been geared at decreasing turnround time to the minimum possible. By 1953 it took $2\frac{1}{2}$ hours for a small ferry with a stern door to unload and reload. By 1962 a drive-through ship carrying 850 passengers and 120 cars could be turned round in $1\frac{1}{2}$ hours. In the year of the tragedy, 1,350 passengers and 350 cars could be turned round in an hour. 'The competition is so intense that crewmen are prepared to ignore any rule just as long as the ferry gets out on time,' commented a National Union of Seamen (NUS) branch official at the time of the Zeebrugge disaster.[13]

Sailing late out of Zeebrugge isn't on

Pressure to leave the berth was identified as one of the underlying reasons why the *Herald*'s crew set sail with the bow doors open. The Sheen inquiry noted 'the sense of urgency to sail at the earliest moment'. It also criticised a memo issued by the operations manager at Zeebrugge in 1986 which urged:

> Put pressure on your first officer if you don't think he is moving fast enough. Have your load ready when the vessel is in and marshall your staff and machines to work efficiently. Let's put the record straight, sailing late out of Zeebrugge isn't on. It's 15 minutes early for us.

This was explained away by the company as 'motivation'. There was presumably no explanation given to the customer who arrived ten minutes before the scheduled departure only to find the ferry disappearing into the distance. The pressure was such that one former Townsend officer said he had known masters and chief officers being asked to explain delays of as little as ten minutes.[14]

At the 1990 criminal trial it was observed that for the ferry company 'sailing on time was regarded as being of the utmost importance'. It was a crucial element in sustaining its competitiveness in a cut-throat market. At the Sheen inquiry, the NUS's representative said: 'Their [Townsend's] primary concern was to carry as much freight and passengers as possible and keep to schedules, with scant regard for safety, particularly where expenditure was involved.'

After Zeebrugge, Viscount Caldecote and Alex Moulton of the Royal Institution of Naval Architects (RINA) commented: 'All those who direct and control great enterprises have a clear responsibility to ensure that their staff are not put under pressure to cut the wrong corners, whether in design or operations.'[15] The trouble came when the pressurised staff had to decide for themselves which were the 'right' corners for them to cut to meet targets, deadlines or schedules.

We cannot charge more than the customer is prepared to pay

Time pressure has played a part in other disasters, as companies have striven to extract the largest quantity of work from their employees – often at the expense of quality. One of the four 'core' causes of the 1988 Clapham rail crash identified by the coroner was time pressure on resignalling around Waterloo. In the USA, an airline and nine of its managers were indicted on charges that supervisors routinely ignored vital repairs and maintenance and then falsified records. The omissions were said to be due to pressure from the airline's headquarters to 'keep the aircraft in flight at all costs'. As a result, employees tried to avoid repairs which would have led to delays or cancellations.

The loss of nearly two hundred lives seemingly had less impact than it should have done on P&O European Ferries' preoccupation with time. In 1988 the *Herald*'s sister ship *Free Enterprise VII* sailed with its bow doors open for a short period. Its captain said, 'I did it and I did wrong. I shouldn't have done, but I was under tremendous pressure.'[16] The nature of the pressure remained unexplained.

Nine months after the disaster, the *Observer* reported that 'crews on cross-Channel ferries are being pressured into hasty turnround of vessels despite safety fears'. Earlier that month, P&O had told its employees: 'We must take early and decisive action to maintain the company's viability. In the fierce competitive area in which we operate, we cannot charge more than the customer is prepared to pay.'[17] The company made no suggestion that customers would be prepared to pay more for im-proved safety or quality of service. That they are prepared to do so was tacitly (though tautologically) supported by the Department of Transport in suggestions to the IMO for increased safety standards. 'It may therefore be necessary to increase revenue, an action which, although unlikely to be welcomed could hardly be criticised by the travelling public if duly informed of the reasons for such an increase,' argued the Department.[18] If the public know that their money is being spent on improved safety they do not begrudge the extra expense.

Vessels are rarely late home on Christmas Eve

A memo leaked to the *Observer*, quoting the P&O European Ferries operations manager Captain D. F. Meredith, further emphasises the company's preoccupation with timing. 'Our present record is now worse than Sealink's and it has become the exception rather than the rule to sail on time,' he wrote late in 1987. 'It is not unreasonable to place everyone under pressure to achieve punctuality as long as no corners are cut and as long as all safety measures are fully observed.'[19]

In response to the *Herald* disaster, the ferry company ensured that lorries were carefully distributed to improve stability. Stringent pre-sailing techniques were introduced to establish the load-line and to ensure bow doors were closed. Though these took time, no extra crew were provided. Despite this, Meredith caustically added, 'Vessels are rarely late home on Christmas Eve.' Jack Bromley of the sea officers' union Numast commented: 'How disingenuous to say you can put pressure on the crew without making shortcuts on safety. This is a return to attitudes before the Zeebrugge tragedy.'

Timing remains a crucial element in the competitiveness of cross-Channel ferry companies. It is widely acknowledged. 'The economic viability of the car ferry industry depends greatly on maximum utilisation of vessels, which in turn is largely dependent on short turnrounds, unimpeded traffic flows of many types of vehicle through vehicle decks, with flexible vehicle stowage arrangements,' said D. R. M. Barwell, technical director of Sealink, in 1987.[20]

'Speed of operation now seems to hold the key to profitability of ferry services,' wrote John Spouge of RINA after the disaster. 'Crews are undoubtedly under pressure to complete the loading and unloading as fast as possible. Similarly the master is reluctant to reduce speed in rough weather or when passing other ships in port approaches.'[21] The masters and officers of the *Titanic* had such an attitude – that was 80 years before.

References

1. *British Social Attitudes 1988–89*, Gower, p. 115.
2. *The Director*, February 1991, p. 66.
3. *Lloyd's List*, 19 December 1987.
4. *Lloyd's List*, 10 April 1991.
5. *The Daily Telegraph*, 10 March 1987.
6. *The Financial Times*, 10 October 1987.
7. *The Story of P&O*, Weidenfeld & Nicholson, 1986, p. 205.
8. *The Financial Times*, 28 February 1990.
9. *Observer*, 27 December 1987.
10. *Naval Architect*, February 1989.
11. *Naval Architect*, April 1987.
12. House of Commons, 24 July 1987 (*Hansard*, p. 686).
13. *The Financial Times*, 10 March 1987.
14. *The Sunday Times*, 15 March 1987.
15. *The Times*, 2 June 1987.
16. *Daily Mirror*, 13 May 1988.
17. *Observer*, 27 December 1987.
18. UK submission to IMO, 4 January 1991.
19. *Observer*, 27 December 1987.
20. *Passenger Ro-Ro Ferry Safety: an Owner's Viewpoint*, D. R. M. Barwell, Second Kummerman International Conference on Ro-Ro Safety and Vulnerability, April 1991.
21. *The Safety of Ro-Ro Passenger Ferries*, J. R. Spouge, RINA spring meeting, 1988.

CHAPTER THREE

THE FAILURE OF DESIGN

'The Government do not accept that these ships
are inherently unsafe … They are not intrinsically unsafe.'
– Lord Brabazon, Minister for Aviation and Shipping.

'… the vulnerability of roll-on ferries is not acceptable.
Things could be done to make these ships safer'
– Viscount Caldecote of RINA.

The rapidity of the *Herald*'s capsize in a calm sea raised questions about
the vulnerability of ro-ro ferries. P&O tried to allay any doubts. 'These
ferries are very stable. Even in a force ten gale there is little rolling,' said
a company spokesman soon after the disaster.[1] This comment drew a
critical response from *New Scientist* magazine:

> He got the story exactly the wrong way round. A bobbing cork
> might be uncomfortable to sit on, but it does not sink.
>   In the case of the *Herald*, the road to disaster probably started
> when the ferry left port without any precise knowledge of the
> stability of the ship after the cargo had been loaded. The quick
> turnaround required by ferry operators at Channel ports means that
> there is little time for making the required calculations, even if the
> weight of the vehicles and their distribution are known. With vehi-
> cle decks full, the weight would be fairly high up in the boat,
> reducing stability.[2]

Again, the importance of speed was cited as an influential factor in the
capsize.

Two inches of water was sufficient to destabilise the ship

Jack Brown, designer of the Neatstow bow doors fitted to the *Herald*,
provided an analogy for the layman:

If you take a cup of water, you can swirl it around without spilling anything. Put it into a saucer and you would have difficulty in moving it even gently around as you wish. But if you put it into a plate you'd be lucky to pick it up without spillage.[3]

Other comments were more disturbing. A former Townsend master went on the record to say that 'just two inches of water [on the car deck] was sufficient to destabilise the ship'.[4]

The operations at Zeebrugge required the *Herald* to pump water into ballast tanks in its bow. This lowered the level of the ship by three feet. As there was only one ramp at Zeebrugge and the *Herald* had two main vehicle decks, the process of unloading and loading took longer than at other ports. At Calais, for example, both decks could be unloaded or loaded simultaneously from two ramps. There had been complaints about the effects of the weight of the water ballast on the ship's handling. At full speed, or even reduced speed, the bow wave sometimes came three-quarters of the way up the bow doors. A vessel 'trimmed' down at the bow does not manoeuvre well. Masters had complained that the ship's ability to stay upright in the event of a collision or incident could be affected by the combination of unknown freight overloading and the bow being low in the water because of the water ballast.

There was a solution to this problem. A Townsend Thoresen chief engineer made repeated requests to the management to install a high-capacity ballast pump which could pump all the bow tanks' water ballast out of the ship before leaving the dock. The existing pump took 90 minutes to empty the tanks. This meant the ship could not get back on to an even keel until it was well out to sea. The new pump would have cost £25,000. This was regarded by the company as prohibitive: the requests were rejected.

The basic design premise behind ro-ros is a commercial one

Other design enhancements would have improved the *Herald*'s stability without increasing fares dramatically. In 1988, the Granada television programme *World in Action* examined the costs of improving the stability of ro-ros. It commissioned a leading firm of naval engineers and architects, MacGregor-Navire, to calculate costs. The firm estimated that installing two sets of steel transverse bulkhead doors would keep ferries afloat for at least 30 minutes, providing vital extra time to save lives after a collision or other mishap. The cost of £115,000 per ferry would have involved a minimum of 28p extra on fares and a maximum of 72p if the company wanted to recover the money in a year.

'The fitting of transverse bulkhead doors to existing ro-ro passenger vessels significantly improves their ability to survive damage or flooding,' said the MacGregor-Navire report. 'The total cost of fitting and using such doors is not negligible, but when considered as an addition to ticket prices, the costs are very small.' For a company like P&O the costs are insubstantial when related to a turnover of £2,920.2 million in 1987. Ferry operators had regarded such bulkheads as unnecessary and as impediments to rapid turnround. When ro-ros were used in the Falklands War of 1982, the Royal Navy installed them. They were taken out when the ships were returned to commercial use.

The basic design premise behind ro-ros is a commercial one. A ro-ro ferry is essentially a raft over which superstructures are built. The economics of their design require that cargo decks are large and there are no bulkheads to divide the space. The fewer divides there are, the easier it is to load and unload vehicles; also more can be carried. As ferries have increased in size this basically commercial structure has remained. No one seems to have questioned the safety implications.

Preserving that basic design was something that, until recently, the Department of Transport thought worth fighting for at the IMO. In 1984 its contribution to an IMO discussion on ferry stability emphasised the importance of commercial considerations. 'Too high a standard [of stability] would effectively place an impossible restriction on designs currently in vogue,' argued the British representative. 'It cannot be emphasised too strongly that to impose the same residual stability criteria on passenger ships ... would place very severe commercial constraints upon them.'[5] The department regarded substantial modifications to the ferry fleet as an unwanted competitive hindrance. It took the Zeebrugge disaster, pressure by the Herald Families Association and RINA, and the irrefutable results of its £1 million research programme to change the department's tune.

With hindsight it is easy to recognise that as ro-ro ferries became larger so did the vulnerability arising from their undivided car decks. But with more and more operators gearing their budgets to the fast turnrounds made possible by this basic design, ethically motivated naval architects found it increasingly difficult to get anyone to heed the concerns they were expressing. Ship owners, successive governments, the Department of Transport, classification societies, insurers and naval architects have all acquiesced in an incremental approach to ro-ro ferry design. Instead of being questioned, the basic design has been enhanced and added to.

This narrow approach had been criticised before Zeebrugge. In 1986, for example, the late Professor Richard Bishop, vice-chancellor and principal of Brunel University and a naval architect, said:

> The annual loss of ships at sea has neither abated nor provoked avowals of deep concern among naval architects. On the contrary, naval architects continue to assure the world (and themselves) that the sea's very unpredictability and occasional ferocity ensure that 'there will always be losses'.[6]

Bishop claimed there was 'an urgent need for lateral thinking in ship research' and suggested that the emphasis on increasing the size of established designs could not continue if the basic precepts were incorrect. 'Naval architecture research is ultimately bound up with the refinement of rules and if the rules are qualitatively wrong they cannot be got right by quantitive adjustments.' Bigger did not mean better, or safer.

Is the level of risk acceptable?

An even blunter plea to naval architects came after the disaster from Maurice de Rohan OBE of the Herald Families Association. Addressing an RINA seminar in December 1987, he said:

> Is the level of risk acceptable? Do you, when you go home at night, feel comfortable that you have done everything to make that risk acceptable to the customers, the passenger, who travel on the ferries? I think there is only one answer: I get a strong feeling that most of the people here would share that answer that it is not acceptable.

But it was not only the personnel involved in ferry design who were questioned and implored to act differently: the very nature of the design process and its organisation was being examined.

Part of the design problem with ferries is that ships are generally built to one-off designs or in small classes. In shipbuilding there are no runs of several hundred products in the way there are in most other transport industries, including aviation. Another difference between the maritime and aviation industries is that while planes can be grounded and modified in their hundreds if a design fault is detected, ferries cannot because their designs and specifications are rarely identical. From a management point of view, solving a design fault is therefore a logistical nightmare at the very least, and very likely to be considered impossible.

The dangers of the incremental approach were demonstrated in another industry by the 1974 explosion at the Flixborough chemical plant. Twenty-nine people died after a modification destroyed the integrity of what was essentially a soundly designed plant.

The best ship to maximise the operator's profits

Incremental design has another implication. According to Richard Goss of the University of Wales Department of Maritime Studies, 'Ship designs often involve extensive testing of models in towing tanks, but that is largely to study hydrodynamic resistance, powering, fuel consumption, seakeeping and manoeuvrability, not safety, and certainly not the safety of life as such. The object, however, is generally the improvement of a particular design.'[7] In other words, once the first principle of the design has been accepted, developments of it are simply aimed at improving performance and capacity. Perhaps the crudest manifestation of this ill-founded concept is the 'jumboisation' of an existing ro-ro ferry by literally cutting it in half and welding a new section into the middle.

This trend, which blurred the need to re-examine the basis of ro-ro ferry design, has been intensified by the financial pressures on the shipping industry, which has been declining for many years. Such pressures discourage innovation. A departure from the basic ro-ro design or principle would have required a costly investment and brought with it greater commercial risk. Designers, anxious for work, provided what the operators demanded. Ferry operators, for their part, regarded ro-ros as an ideal solution, giving them both speed and size. Once the basic design was in use, there seemed to be no going back. Admitting to concerns about the fundamental stability of the ships would hardly have endeared naval architects to the people they depend on for a living, the ship operators. Ferry operators could ask why, if the design of ro-ros was fallible, naval architects continued designing them. The very fact that naval architects had designed such ships was used as an argument for their safety – even after RINA had publicly voiced its concerns and 192 people had died after a simple human error.

In the House of Lords, maritime author Lord Greenway commented in March 1988:

> There seems to be slightly more evidence now to suggest that under certain circumstances a ro-ro might not be quite so stable as an ordinary compartmented merchant ship. However, be that as it may, the roll-on roll-off ships operating today have been built and designed by these self-same naval architects to the latest internationally recognised standards. The operators and shipowners have confidence in them ... Passengers still have confidence in them.

The ro-ro design was favoured because it travelled quickly through the water and spent the minimum time possible in port. 'The naval architects decided on a design that was relatively difficult to build. They wanted the best ship to maximise the operator's profits,' said *New Scientist* magazine in the month of the disaster. The speed of the *Herald* and its sister ships was well proven. One of them had averaged 23.9 knots in a crossing between Dover and Calais in 1980. This was the fastest-ever ferry crossing between the two ports and took place in a force 8 gale.

Despite the commercial attractiveness of the design, in the years preceding the Zeebrugge disaster the stability and safety of ro-ro ferries was increasingly questioned. In many quarters it continues to be.

Exceptionally vulnerable to human error

When she visited Zeebrugge immediately after the disaster, the then Prime Minister Margaret Thatcher said: 'It is the fundamental design of the ferry that, I understand, is the problem. That is a factor that will have to be looked at very quickly because public confidence has been severely jolted.'[8] It was a point supported by a Department of Transport spokesman who said it was 'well-known' that ro-ros had design problems.[9] Only a couple of days later, the then Transport Secretary John Moore offered a considerably different view of ro-ro safety. On 9 March 1987, he told the House of Commons: 'I have no evidence to support the view that this was due to any fault in the design of the ship.'

The transformed governmental view ignored a large weight of research and opinion. Over five years prior to Zeebrugge, *Freight News* had a lead story entitled 'Ro-ro ships unstable'. 'When ro/ro means "roll-on, roll-over"' was the headline of a chillingly prescient article in *Shipcare* in the month before the *Herald* capsized. 'Move to make ro-ro ships more safe' ran a story in the *Journal of Commerce*. More dramatically, *The Sunday Times* proclaimed 'The ships that sink with an inch of water' in 1981. 'Rethink on watertight doors' announced *Lloyd's List* in 1985.[10]

As far back as 1981 a meeting of the Institute of London Underwriters had expressed the 'urgent need for extra safety factors to be built into ro-ros'. Insurance companies were so concerned they actually added a surcharge to insurance premiums for ro-ros.[11] In the aftermath of Zeebrugge, a variety of warnings by maritime experts about ro-ro ferries was easily uncovered. In 1986, for example, the IMO had given a warning that ro-ros were exceptionally vulnerable to human error.

The list of doubters was long. They did not apparently include ship owners and operators, who expressed a different view. 'Any suggestion that the design of the ships is at fault or that the Department of Transport or ferry operators have refused to correct design deficiencies is ... non-sense,' said James Sherwood, chairman of Sealink, after Zeebrugge.[12] In fact, the chances of a ferry capsizing were put by Lloyd's Register as one every five years in a risk analysis undertaken at the request of the Department of Transport. In total there were 5,300 passengers killed in 245 'serious incidents' involving ro-ro ferries worldwide between 1978 and 1988, making travelling by ferry ten times as dangerous as civil aviation.[13]

Concerns continue to be voiced. The report into the fire on the ferry *Scandinavian Star* in 1990, in which 148 people died, concluded: 'There remains a significant risk of a single incident resulting in several hundred fatalities. There is also some circumstantial evidence ... to suggest that this risk is increasing.'[14] The day before the disaster, Swedish unions had called the ferry 'unacceptably dangerous'.

Before Zeebrugge, the worst British disaster involving a ro-ro was in 1953, when the *Princess Victoria* sank in the Irish Sea, killing 134. The world's worst ferry disaster had been in 1981, when 431 died on an Indonesian ferry which caught fire and sank in the Java Sea.

The large, unprotected space of a ro-ro ferry vehicle deck – only a few feet above the waterline – is not divided, and therefore protected, in the way the hull of a conventional ship is divided. The weaknesses of this critical departure from traditional naval architecture were exposed well over a hundred years ago. In 1854, the troopship *Birkenhead* sank off Africa because its bulkheads had been removed to enable cavalry officers to exercise their horses. Some five hundred people died including many women and children and the disaster led to a Shipping Act which stipulated that iron vessels over 100 tons should have divided hulls. Ship owners regarded this as a 'mischievous piece of legislation' as it made it more difficult to load ships. Their powerful lobby ensured it was soon repealed. Over a century later, the *Herald* was allowed to sail without bulkheads on the car deck. It weighed 8,000 tons.

As if the statistical evidence of ro-ro deficiencies was not worrying enough, in roughly two-thirds of the cases the capsize took less than five minutes. In an incident somewhat similar to the Zeebrugge disaster, a ro-ro capsized and sank within minutes in the River Yarra in Melbourne, Australia, in 1974. It was reversing into berth with its stern door open. An inquiry into the incident made strong recommendations about the opening and closing of the doors.

If ro-ro ships do capsize and are not fortuitously in shallow water at the time, very high fatality levels must follow

---

The other ro-ro ships which have sunk rapidly as a result of a collision include the *Jolly Azzurro* (1978), *Collo* (1980), *Tollan* (1980), *Sloman Ranger* (1980), *Ems* (1981), *European Gateway* (1982) and *Mont Louis* (1984). In 1988 a Finnish ro-ro freighter, *Ra*, loaded with beer, sank 28 miles from land. According to Dutch coastguards, it went down like a stone. There was no time to put out a Mayday call; only by chance were the crew found in their liferafts. In 1989 the ferry *Hamburg*, crossing the North Sea, was struck by a container ship which ripped a 20-metre gash above and below the waterline. Three passengers died but, fortunately, the master was alert to the danger and adjusted the vessel's trim tanks, causing it to heel away from the hole and prevent water from entering.[15] The rapidity of the capsize was why some five hundred passengers – over two-thirds of the total – died when the *Salem Express* sank in the Red Sea on 14 December 1991 after striking a coral reef. To those concerned with passenger safety, the mounting roll of ro-ro ferry disasters should have been disturbing long before the *Herald*'s capsize made it impossible for them to go on ignoring this hazard.

Over the years a variety of research programmes and papers confirmed the design deficiencies of ro-ros. In 1978 det Norske Veritas, the Norwegian ship classification bureau and a world authority on ship stability, warned that ro-ros without watertight bulkheads in their vehicle decks could capsize in two minutes. It concluded that 'total losses as a result of collision are much higher for ro-ros'[16] and that 60 per cent of ro-ro losses capsized or sunk in less than ten minutes. One of the authors of the bureau's report on ro-ros, Michael Huther, commented after the Zeebrugge disaster that he was 'shocked but not surprised'[17] by the speed of the *Herald*'s capsize.

In March 1981 *International Shipbuilding Progress* published the results of a Polish study into ro-ro safety.[18] They showed that in 95 per cent of collisions involving smaller ro-ros on short sea journeys and in not less than 70 per cent of larger, ocean-going incidents, the main vehicle deck would become immersed in water. In effect, the results anticipated what would happen with the *Herald of Free Enterprise*. After the disaster, Dr Pawlowski of the Gdansk Ship Research Institute, a member of its research team, warned: 'If nothing is done to increase the fundamental safety of ro-ro ships, another disaster similar to Zeebrugge is only a matter of time.'[19]

Clearly, the quicker a ship sinks after an incident, the less likely people are to survive. Bearing this in mind, passenger ship safety regulations stipulate that a damaged vessel should stay afloat in a near-upright condition for at least 30 minutes. Marshall Meek (former head of technology at British Shipbuilders and managing director of the National Maritime Institute) wrote in the *Seatrade Business Review* a few months after Zeebrugge:

> The concept of a ship capsizing rapidly before personnel can get off is new and constitutes the fundamental difference between ro-ros and all conventional ships since time immemorial. All other ships are designed to give time for personnel on board to be evacuated in emergency and for lifesaving appliances to be deployed. If ro-ro ships do capsize and are not fortuitously in shallow water at the time, very high fatality levels must follow.

Even among the uninitiated, such an apparent lack of stability raises worrying questions. To professional mariners it ought to be a daunting prospect. A former master, Captain J. H. Isherwood, wrote in October 1987:

> It does not require any technical knowledge to see that if an 8,000 ton ship turns upside down in four minutes when water enters right forward through a door six feet to eight feet above the waterline, in mild weather, there is something very radically wrong with the design.[20]

In a letter to *The Daily Telegraph* he went on to label such ferries 'floating death-traps'.

It is downright wicked to stray over the margins of safety just to 'pack them in'

Other experienced mariners have similar reservations about the basic design of ro-ros. In a letter to *The Times* in March 1986, Commander Robert Wall, for example, pointed to the fact that bow and stern doors are there simply because they reduce turnround time and increase the frequency of sailings. 'It is bad enough to create the ugliest ships in maritime history,' he commented, 'but downright wicked to stray over the margins of safety just to "pack them in" in the interests of profit margins.'

Ferry operators may protest that it is easy to identify hazards with hindsight. They would have difficulty in substantiating this argument in view of the widely publicised evidence that ro-ros were liable to capsize very rapidly when their watertight integrity was breached. Perhaps the most powerful illustration of their blinkered thinking is the familiar photograph of the stricken *Herald* lying on its side festooned with traditional lifeboats which could not be launched. The Sheen report confirmed suspicions about the inherent inability of ro-ro vessels to sustain damage and remain afloat long enough for passengers and crew to escape. It recommended that research be undertaken into various design changes which would improve ro-ro ferry damage survival.

The results of commercial interest ...

Townsend Thoresen had already experienced the fallibility of ro-ros at first hand. In 1982 its ferry *European Gateway* capsized with the loss of six lives after a collision with Sealink's *Speedlink Vanguard* in the approaches to the port of Harwich. It capsized in four minutes. This provoked speculation about the damage stability of ro-ro ferries. Like the *Herald*, the *European Gateway* came to rest on its side half-submerged in shallow water, narrowly avoiding a deep-water sinking with heavy loss of life. Luckily it only had 70 passengers and crew on board. Despite the loss of 192 lives, the *Herald* was similarly fortunate. If it had not suddenly veered towards starboard, where the sandbanks lay, many more people would have died. The formal report into the 1982 capsize gloomily concluded: 'It cannot be satisfactory to proceed upon the basis that no passenger vessel will ever again suffer a fate similar to that of the *European Gateway.*' Guarded though the language was, the undercurrent of worry was clear.

Not surprisingly, the *Gateway* capsize made Townsend examine passenger safety. The resulting report observed:

> The company and ship's master could be considered negligent on the following points, particularly when some are the results of 'commercial interest':
> a. The ship's draught is not read before sailing, and the draught entered into the official log book is completely erroneous;
> b. It is not standard practice to inform the master of his passenger figures before sailing;
> c. The tonnage of cargo is not declared to the master before sailing;
> d. Full speed is maintained in dense fog.

'Commercial interests', therefore, were identified by the company as contributing to the mistakes which caused the capsize. But lessons, however dutifully recorded, are not necessarily learned.

P&O European Ferries' miscalculation of the Zeebrugge casualties showed that point (b) was not observed. The Sheen inquiry also found that, with the apparent knowledge of the Department of Transport, inaccurate draught readings were regularly entered in the *Herald*'s log book. This was because the design of that class of vessels made it impossible to ascertain the draught by the crude, conventional method. The company had not installed draught gauge indicators which would have made measurement practical.

Technical solutions are available now. The means of their enforcement are not

---

The *European Gateway* set off a lively debate among naval architects. 'Let us hope that we do not have to wait for a major disaster involving a ro-ro passenger before the design is improved,' commented one member of the RINA in 1986.[21] Nevertheless, both funds and interest in seeking design solutions were limited. In November 1986 an appeal from British Maritime Technology for money to research safety aspects of ro-ros was spurned by every ferry operator. Its quarter-mile-long towing tank and a £2 million multi-directional wave and manoeuvrability tank had to be mothballed. The loss of six people on the *European Gateway* failed to shake the shipping industry or stir politicians into action. 'I am appalled to realise now that no effective action was taken after the *European Gateway* capsize,' lamented RINA president Viscount Caldecote, in 1988.

At Townsend, responsibility for the design and construction of new vessels rested with technical director Wallace Ayers, though he admitted at the committal proceedings that he 'did not care for the title'. He had been responsible for the design and construction of the *Herald*. One of his responsibilities was to 'approve modifications to existing ships' and, presumably, to consider whether the design implications of the *European Gateway* capsize were implemented. Tellingly, Ayers' objectives were said to be to 'analyse requirements for ships' design and ensure that ships are available and disposed to make profits'.

One simple design modification could have saved the *Herald*. Standing on the bridge, the ship's master could not see if the bow doors were closed or open. An indicator light would simply, and cheaply, have allowed him to check. Since 1984 all new-built ferries have had to have a light on the bridge to indicate that the bow doors are open. According to Numast, Townsend declined requests from representatives of the *Herald*'s crew to have one installed. Various masters had also asked for them to be fitted in the older vessels. Indicator lights had been used in some ferries since the early 1970s. However, little attempt was made to ensure that design modifications incorporated in newly built ships were introduced into the existing fleet; that was said to be an expensive process.

The vulnerability of roll-on ferries is not acceptable

At the Sheen inquiry, Townsend's marine superintendent Jeffrey Develin was asked, 'Didn't it strike you as obvious that what was required in a new building ship was also required in one that was going to be running for another 15 years?' Develin replied, 'No. It should have done.' Indicator lights were eventually fitted to all ro-ros after the Zeebrugge disaster, yet a television programme over a year later included allegations that the lights were not in fact working – even after the 1 January 1988 deadline when the Department of Transport required them to do so. P&O's response (in a press release on 3 May 1988) was that indicator lights had been fitted to the bow and stern doors of all the company's vessels in March and April 1987 with the approval of local Department of Transport inspectors but were subsequently amended 'at the first opportunity' to comply with a specification revised by the Department 'in the light of experience'.

The fact is, safety standards and design modifications lag behind technological advances. It is not perhaps inevitable, but it is certainly reality. This highlights the fact that the onus must be on the operators themselves to reach the highest possible standards of design and safety. The gap between regulation and practice was demonstrated when high-speed catamarans, carrying 450 people, were introduced between Dover and France. Safety regulations to cover such vessels were not to be introduced for another three years. The RINA's Professor Ken Rawson warned: 'These catamarans are being introduced all over the world. They are very lightweight, flimsy craft. The problem is the new regulations will come too late.'

The Department of Transport candidly admitted: 'It's a problem of new technology outstripping old regulations. We need a code that is more suitable for high-performance vessels – we are working as fast as we can.'[22] The operators, not surprisingly, stressed that they were adhering to regulations. 'We are aware that new rulings for these crafts are being discussed. But we are operating to the existing standards with the backing of the Department of Transport,' said Hoverspeed.[23]

A similar gulf between the regulatory world and reality existed in 1987. Despite widespread misgivings about ro-ro ferries, the *Herald* adhered to safety standards. No serious offence was committed under maritime law and regulations on 6 March 1987.

There are ways of making these ships safer

After Zeebrugge, the RINA (with six thousand members worldwide) established an in-house technical committee to investigate ro-ro stability. A year after the disaster it submitted proposals on ro-ro design to the government. In a statement weighed down with caution, the RINA president, Viscount Caldecote, said:

> We recognise there is no such thing as absolute safety, but the vulnerability of roll-on ferries is not acceptable. Things could be

done to make these ships safer, although solutions are not easy to find.

It would be foolish to rush in and do something that would not be fully effective, but we believe this is an urgent matter and we want action as soon as possible. Technical solutions to the fundamental problem of rapid capsize following flooding are available now. The means of their enforcement are not. It is indisputable that their implementation will cost money, but safety must over-ride such considerations.[24]

The General Council of British Shipping (GCBS), the representative body of ship owners, retorted that it thought RINA had oversimplified the issues. RINA's comments were supported by another maritime body, the Nautical Institute. It too felt that the vulnerability of ro-ros had to some extent been masked by their generally good safety record. It argued that vulnerability was, in fact, a different issue from safety, dealing as it does with a ship's ability to survive an accident rather than the prevention of one. As Caldecote observed, the solutions were there for all to see; the will to enforce them, however, was clearly not.

After the disaster, Marshall Meek lamented: 'There are ways of making these ships safer and we should be thinking urgently about what to do, not discussing alternatives interminably.'[25] Even discussion was sometimes too much to ask for. Lord Brabazon, then Minister for Aviation and Shipping, told the House of Lords during a debate on the new Merchant Shipping Bill on 10 November 1987: 'The Government do not accept that these ships are inherently unsafe ... They are not intrinsically unsafe. They are unsafe only if a large volume of water enters them on the car deck, and this should be normally well above the waterline.' But political phrase-making is no substitute for safety.

One of the recommendations of the Sheen inquiry was that 'immediate consideration should be given to phasing out vessels built under 1965 rules [for the stability of passenger ships] unless they meet or can be modified to meet, at least, the 1980 standards ...' It was March 1989 before the Department of Transport completed its survey and reported that 17 out of a total of 72 British ferries did not meet the 1980 standards, and that six of them could not be modified. At first, the department refused to name the six, giving 'commercial sensitivity' as the reason for not doing so. P&O, to its credit, revealed that they included two of its vessels, the *Pride of Hythe* and the *Pride of Canterbury*, both operating on the Dover–Boulogne route. It omitted to mention a third, the *St Ola*, which was still running between Scrabster and Stromness in Orkney at the end of 1991, though due to be replaced in March 1992.[26] The department eventually yielded to public pressure and identified all six vessels – but only after their names had been published by the media.

Current international standards are not sufficient

The clearest governmental response to concern was a £1 million research programme into 'stability and related safety aspects' of ro-ros. At the end of October 1987, its steering committee was established. When asked what its terms of reference were, the Department of Transport replied, 'Details haven't been finalised yet.' The eight-man committee included four civil servants, an academic, a union representative and two members from the shipping industry (one from the GCBS and one from P&O). This provided for a greater degree of independence than the programme set up by the shipping operators to examine similar issues, which was carried out by Three Quays, a P&O subsidiary, and Hart Fenton, a Sealink subsidiary.

Early in 1990, when the government's research programme into ro-ros was completed, the Department of Transport admitted: 'The biggest problem confronting ministerial efforts to improve safety remains the cost of structural improvements and a reluctance by other seafaring nations to endorse tighter international standards.'[27] Again cost is given as one of only two impediments to improved safety standards. That such improvements are necessary was candidly admitted by the department. 'Current international standards are not sufficient to rule out the possibility of capsize in respect of existing ferries,' it said before conceding the need for tighter regulations. 'All existing ferries which operate in and out of UK ports should be required to comply with a higher standard of damage stability.' A government adviser on ro-ros added: 'They are most definitely towards the end of the acceptable safety spectrum.'[28]

New damage stability standards for ro-ro ferries were introduced internationally in April 1990 but were restricted to vessels built after that date. At the end of 1990 only two of the ferries in the existing UK fleet met them. Both of these belonged to Sealink. In January 1991 the Department of Transport unveiled a new safety improvement programme. It proposed that the latest damage stability standards – known as SOLAS 90 – should be applied retrospectively to existing vessels and that those that could not be brought up to them should be phased out over an agreed period. The department estimated that the necessary modifications would cost a total of £50–60 million for the 40 ro-ros operating on international routes and £20–25 million for the 17 on domestic routes. Operational costs would increase by £10 million a year for the international fleet and by £2 million for the domestic fleet.[29] Though substantial, these costs had to be weighed against profits averaging about £5 million per vessel per year.

The department submitted its recommendations to the IMO, calling for 'urgent consideration and application'. It proposed that all existing ferries should comply with the IMO's 1990 regulations for damage stability. It also suggested the necessary changes should be completed by May 1993 and said it was prepared to take unilateral action. Those in the shipping industry anticipated fare increases. Jim Hannah, director of communications for the Sealink Stena Line, said dismissively: 'This is a preliminary document which has been hurriedly put together.'[30]

Early in 1991, the IMO accepted the British proposals. It did so, however, with an important caveat: the 1990 standards would not apply to the older vessels until 1994 and then their owners would be allowed five years to make the necessary alterations. The Department of Transport claimed a political victory and conveniently forgot its threat of unilateral action and its suggested implementation date of May 1993.

The following year the IMO watered down the measures agreed earlier by extending the modification period by six years and allowing compliance with SOLAS 90 to take place in phases ranging from less than 70 per cent by 1 October 1994 to 90–5 per cent by 1 October 2005 (more than seventeen years after the *Herald*'s capsize!). The UK, along with Ireland, reserved its position on this absurd decision and set out to gain regional acceptance of the original proposals.

Some experts warned that the British climb-down made another disaster all the more likely. Dr Ewan Corlett, one of the assessors at the Sheen inquiry, said:

> The danger is that if there is a collision – a right-angled collision – a fully loaded ship of the present type has very little chance of survival. You are in a not dissimilar position to an aircraft falling out of the sky, because if you get a lot of water on the vehicle deck you will get an instantaneous or virtually instantaneous capsize. The chances of passengers getting off are very slim indeed. This will happen sooner or later.

A unique leisure environment

The next era of cross-Channel ferries will pose design problems as ships become larger and larger. P&O has plans for four new super ferries as part of a £200 million investment in new ships. The first, *European Seaway*, launched in April 1991, is two and a half times the size of the *Herald*, at 20,000 tons. Sealink has similar ambitions. Its then chairman, James Sherwood, has promised: 'We will be creating a unique leisure environment for passengers.'[31] Its ferry, *Fantasia*, carries 1,800 passengers as well as 723 cars or 107 articulated lorries. It even includes a 'sky dome disco'. The next generation of ships may be even larger. The *Silja Serenade* on the Stockholm–Helsinki route carries 2,500 passengers and has a conference centre with room for six hundred people.

Ferries already in operation are being greatly enlarged – the *Pride of Kent* (formerly the *Spirit of Free Enterprise*) has been increased in size from 8,000 to 20,000 tons so it will be able to carry 1,800, rather than 474, passengers. Increases in capacity bring financial savings. One estimate is that super ferries will reduce operational costs by 40 per cent. More generally, the result of such technological developments is clear: responsibilities on designers, crews and operators will grow ever larger. The capacity of legislators and regulators to keep pace with rapidly increasing technology, as well as accepting their share of responsibility, must remain open to question.

The instability issue was almost wholly eliminated from the criminal trial. Defence counsel were able to state, without contradiction, that 'no-one suggests the design of the vessels was at fault'. Even so, weaknesses in ro-ro design were well publicised. Lay observers could be forgiven for thinking this issue had a great deal of bearing on the company's responsibility to design a better system to ensure that the most critical operation on a ro-ro ferry was carried out than the one which failed on 6 March 1987.

References

1. *New Scientist*, 12 March 1987.
2. Ibid.
3. *The Daily Telegraph*, 10 March 1987.
4. *The Sunday Times*, 15 March 1987.
5. IMO Sub-committee on Stability and Load Lines and on Fishing Vessels Safety, 30th Session, 17 January 1985.
6. *Naval Architect*, July/August 1986.
7. 'Legislation, regulation and enforcement: shipping', Richard Goss, paper presented at Royal Aeronautical Society/RINA Conference on Safety at Sea and in the Air: Taking Stock Together, 1990.
8. *New Scientist*, 12 March 1987.
9. Ibid.
10. *The Sunday Times*, 15 March 1987.
11. *The Sunday Time*s, 1 February 1987.
12. *The Times*, 23 May 1987.
13. *Guardian*, 20 October 1990.
14. *The Sunday Times*, 15 April 1990.
15. *New Scientist*, 9 February 1991.
16. 'Focus on the IMO', IMO paper, May 1986.
17. Ibid.
18. *The Engineer*, March 1987.
19. *Lloyd's List*, 20 November 1987.
20. *The Daily Telegraph*, 14 October 1987.
21. *Naval Architect*, March 1986.
22. *Independent on Sunday*, 7 July 1991.
23. *Observer*, 7 July 1991.
24. *The Daily Telegraph*, 22 March 1988.
25. *Guardian*, 10 October 1988.
26. *Wavelength*, P&O magazine, October 1991.
27. Report of the Steering Committee of the Ro-Ro Ferry Safety Research Programme, HMSO, 1990.
28. Ibid.
29. Department of Transport press notice, 25 January 1991.
30. *The Times*, 26 January 1991.
31. *Dover Express*, 7 July 1989.

CHAPTER FOUR

COMMITMENT TO SAFETY

'The responsibility of trying to ensure that accidents don't
happen is obviously a responsibility of management.'
– Jeffrey Sterling, P&O chairman.

'The first consideration of the Master and of every Officer and
Rating must be the safety of the ship and the lives of the people on
board.'
– P&O fleet regulations.

'Safety: the state of being safe; exemption from hurt or injury; freedom
from danger; the quality of being unlikely to cause hurt or injury;
freedom from dangerousness; the ratio between the strains put upon any
material and the ultimate strength of the material.'
– *Shorter Oxford English Dictionary.*

'The board of directors did not appreciate their responsibility for safety on
their ships,' said the Sheen report on the disaster. Others had a different
view. 'There is human error factor in everything and that is what happened in this case,' claimed Peter Ford, chairman of P&O European
Ferries. He expressed his complete satisfaction with ro-ro safety, despite
the loss of 192 lives. 'Normally the ferries are a safe form of transport. But
like anything else accidents can happen. Many millions of people travel in
them. They are obviously very safe,' he said a month after the Zeebrugge
disaster.[1]

It is too tempting ... to quickly blame human error

In such situations, claims of human error are all too convenient. But it is
difficult to see how one man alone can be responsible for a disaster in a
complex transport operation. The human error is more likely to involve a

number of people over a period of time than simply to be a momentary lapse by an individual. Maritime safety expert Professor Chengi Kuo of Strathclyde University argues: 'Most accidents are not caused by one single factor but up to 12 to 20 factors. If they are activated together you stand a greater risk.'

Research in 1991 by the Department of Transport (published in *The Human Element in Shipping Casualties*) showed that a 'human element was found to be present in over 90 per cent of collisions and groundings, and in over 70 per cent of contacts and fires/explosions.'[2]

The British Health and Safety Executive's (HSE) accident prevention unit has calculated that human error contributes to about 90 per cent of accidents but that 70 per cent are preventable. It argues that the way a company is organised is 'critical in determining employees' behaviour. The prime requirement is a visible commitment to safety from the most senior members of the organisation so that a management culture is developed which promotes a climate for safety.' Few would dispute that emphasis on top-level commitment, though many would put the 'preventable' proportion of accidents much higher. The HSE report goes on to say that if safety is not regarded as an issue of prime importance, employees may be unwilling to follow good safety procedures for fear of being criticised or even disciplined; and that, where priorities are confused, safety is likely to come into conflict with commercial pressures.

Sloppiness at the top leads to sloppiness down the line

The lead must come from the top. Robert McKee, chairman of Conoco UK, is one senior manager who has got the message. 'It's silly to ask any employee of any enterprise to value and pursue a particular objective, especially an over-riding one, if they can't see a genuine and total dedication to safety from the top,' he says. The dedication cannot be half-hearted or short lived, but needs constant refinement and reinforcement. 'Like all disciplines, safe practices have to be learnt and impressed,' says Captain Warren Leback, a fellow of the Nautical Institute. 'Once a company loses its commitment to safety standards, it loses its ability to contain risk.'

David MacIntosh, a defence lawyer involved in the *Piper Alpha*, Bradford City football stadium and other disaster cases, says:

It is too tempting, even for corporations who ought to know better, to quickly blame human error. It is simpler to blame the error of some individual in the front line than to wish to analyse the short-comings of your own corporate design and your own corporate safety procedures. Nearly all the major incidents involve a series of mistakes, some minor in their individual impact, which in the aggregate lead to the disaster. It is very rare indeed that one simple piece of negligence causes a disaster. Even if it does, it is very rare that the consequences of this disaster flow from that one mistake.[3]

His thoughts are echoed and supported by Maurice de Rohan of the Herald Families Association:

Sloppiness at the top leads to sloppiness down the line. If safety is not an issue at the board level, it is generally seen as unimportant at the operational level. The responsibility of the board of directors is to establish policy, to put in place the right organisation and to review what is happening to ensure its policies are being properly implemented. In management terms, it is not adequate to say I did not know, therefore I cannot be held accountable.

Responsibility for safety lies in the selection, training and motivation of personnel; in the equipment they are given; in the design of systems; and, most importantly, in the creation of a working environment where human errors become less likely. These are all management and board-level responsibilities. Safety is an act of leadership, not of delegation. It is not necessarily a matter of having a rigidly applied safety rulebook – rulebooks encourage the apportioning of blame, whereas a good example by senior management does not.

What happens when management fails to take on this responsibility was shown by a safety audit carried out by health and safety inspectors after six deaths on the British side of the Channel tunnel. Their main criticism was of 'an underlying weakness in safety management, particularly leadership and administration, giving rise to an inadequate safety culture'. The acts and attitude of management had a clearly perceived effect on employees down the line.

At the time of Zeebrugge there was a Department of Transport recommendation on 'good ship management'. It advised that 'the overall responsibility of the shipping company requires the need for close involvement by management ashore. To this end it is recommended that every company operating ships should designate a person ashore with responsibility for monitoring the technical and safety aspects of the operation of its ships.'[4] Within the company operating the *Herald* there was a managerial vacuum when it came to safety. The Department of Transport's advice was ignored.

Later, P&O said: 'Safety is top of the agenda as far as we are concerned.'[5] Sterling also seemed to accept this when he said: 'The responsibility of trying to ensure that accidents don't happen is obviously a responsibility of management.'[6] But at the time of Zeebrugge it was unclear who held responsibility for this crucial aspect of the company's business.

We're all professionals … of course it's safe

At the Sheen inquiry, the company's marine superintendent, Jeffrey Develin, was asked who was responsible for safety. He replied, 'Well in truth, nobody, though there ought to have been.' In general, Townsend's directors did not have specific areas of responsibility. Company standing orders setting out safety responsibilities on ship were ill-defined and vague. This was not altogether surprising since no individual had particular responsibility for ensuring that they were properly drafted.

The Fennell report into the King's Cross fire, in which 31 people died, identified similar confusion as a key cause of that disaster. London Regional Transport believed it had delegated responsibility for safety to its operating companies. But London Underground thought it had assumed responsibility only for the safe operation of the Underground system and not its physical structures. Confusion led to neglect. 'The railway tradition before King's Cross was that safety was part of everyone's job and we're all professionals and of course it's safe. King's Cross showed us that it wasn't,' reflected Denis Tunnicliffe, managing director of London Underground, after the fire.[7] The dilution of responsibility leads, eventually, to no one taking any responsibility.

Put in the best system and review it

The comments of some indicate that a similar malaise may have afflicted the ferry business. No less a person than the president of the Nautical Institute, Commodore Gordon Greenfield, said in 1987: 'Safety has always been a dirty word in the shipping dictionary. It has a negative value and is boring both to sea and shore staff, not to mention passengers.' From a traditional management point of view, there is little to be gained from spending valuable managerial time on safety. It is not a means of rapid career advancement – marketers, financiers and accountants get to the top of the executive tree; safety managers stay where they are. In shipping, as in so many other industries, there is little reward or induce-ment to anyone involved in increasing safety levels. Neither shipbuilders nor operators stand to gain from any additional cost devoted to greater safety or higher standards of operation.

At Townsend, on-shore responsibility for the safety of the *Herald of Free Enterprise*, its crew and passengers was divided between three people. Jeffrey Develin, a director of Townsend since October 1986, was responsible for the safe operation of the company fleet and was supposed to liaise with senior masters. John Kirby, as senior master of the *Herald*, was responsible for the co-ordination of masters and officers to ensure uniformity and safety. As group technical director, Wallace Ayers was responsible for the construction and design of new vessels and improve-ments to old ones. Develin co-ordinated the British end of the rescue and later commented: 'It is not right to blame one individual ... If you have a system where one man's failure automatically leads to disaster it's wrong ... There is no such thing as perfect safety. You put in the best or a very good system and you review it.'[8] Townsend neither installed the best system nor ensured that it was updated in the light of changed operating conditions. For instance, the door-closing procedures were not rewritten when visor doors (clearly visible from the bridge when open) were superseded by 'clam' doors (seen only with great difficulty).

P&O fleet regulations apparently make the company's attitude to safety quite clear:

The first consideration of the Master and of every Officer and Rating must be the safety of the ship and the lives of the people on board. This consideration over-rides all other obligations and in matters of safety the Master has discretion to take whatever action he considers to be in the best interests of the ship. Under no circumstances must schedule, expense, convenience or prior in-structions be allowed to justify the taking of any risk which may endanger the ship or any passenger or member of the ship's com-pany.

The Master must never be persuaded against his better judgement to undertake any operation or manoeuvre which he knows to be unduly hazardous. The Company will always support a decision taken by the Master in good faith and in the interests of safety.

This makes it clear that responsibility rests with one man: the captain. The company, its directors and management are distant figures protected by simply delegating all operational responsibilities to the masters.

The system was inherently unsafe

Despite P&O's bold statement, the safety procedures for which it assumed responsibility when it took over Townsend were far from secure. The Minister for Aviation and Shipping, Lord Brabazon, later observed: 'The tragic consequences of the two major accidents to British ro-ro ferries since the mid-1950s could have been avoided by simple improvements in operational procedures.' Both those disasters involved Townsend vessels. When Captain Lewry appealed against the decision to suspend his master's certificate for a year, the procedures were called 'a non-system looking for a disaster'.

At the criminal trial in 1990, the prosecution counsel said: 'The system was ... inherently unsafe. The orders in force which were supposed to be followed on board the ship were unclear and inadequate.' A general instruction introduced in 1984 proves that point. It required the officer loading the main vehicle deck – G deck – to ensure that the watertight and bow/stern doors were secured when leaving port. Was the *Herald*, less than a mile from the dockside when it capsized, still in the process of 'leaving port'?

In practice, as first officer Leslie Sabel and several masters admitted, the written instruction that the loading officer should check the doors were closed was routinely ignored. It was interpreted merely as a requirement to check that someone was in a position to close them. On the night of the disaster Sabel saw a figure he believed to be the assistant bosun on the car deck and then headed for the bridge, expecting the bow doors to be closed in his absence. No one will ever know how many times vessels left port with their bow doors open and were fortunate enough to avoid disaster. At the time a Belgian shipping journalist commented: 'If every ship sailing out of here with its doors wide open were to sink, we could walk to England across the wrecks.'

The most glaring weakness in the door-closing procedure was that it relied on negative reporting. Although there was a system of positive reporting for tasks such as ensuring the propellers were clear of ropes, portholes were closed and the bow anchors secured, the ship's standing orders made no reference to opening and closing the doors. 'I did not check that the doors were closed because there was a system for that. It had never failed. Not until that night,' Captain Lewry said. In fact, the system was that no news was good news. If the captain heard nothing, he assumed the doors were shut and the ship was ready to sail. It was, Lewry conceded at the Sheen inquiry, 'a very dangerous situation and a very dangerous system'.

Systems must provide for the possibility of human error

The company standing order, 'Ready for sea', was the basis of the negative reporting system:

> Heads of Department are to report to the Master immediately they are aware of any deficiency which is likely to cause their departments to be unready for sea in any respect at the due sailing time. In the absence of any such report the Master will assume, at the due sailing time, that the vessel is ready for sea in all respects.

During the criminal trial, prosecution counsel commented:

> The simplest thing in the world was for the assistant bosun and chief officer to get on the telephone and ring the bridge to say the doors were shut. Had there been such a system in operation – and you can hardly think of anything more basic, elementary and sensible – the master would not have sailed unless he received a positive report.

Sheen said the 'order was unsatisfactory in many respects'. Instead of going through a checklist or even communicating with key staff, it was assumed everything was ready. This was both time saving and easier. It failed on one crucial point – that systems must provide for the possibility of human error, even errors by more than one person.

On ro-ros the human element is crucial. 'What seems to be unique to ro-ro vessels is the extent to which apparently trivial departures from the correct operating procedure or understandable and inevitable human oversights lead to catastrophic accidents,' said RINA member John

Spouge, who was involved in the formal investigation into the capsize of the *European Gateway*.[9] Negative reporting was a flawed procedure. It remained in place on the *Herald* despite the fact that the loading officer's task was more complex on the Zeebrugge run as he had to connect a double-deck ship to the single-level loading ramp. Furthermore, the company's standing orders had not been modified when the number of officers on the Zeebrugge route was reduced. As a result, the loading officer was required to be on the car deck supervising door closure at the same time as he was supposed to be on the bridge overseeing the ship's departure.

Standing orders ... are ignored by the company when it is commercially expedient

---

At the trial, Develin (the man responsible for the safe operation of the fleet) said he was not aware of the contents of the ship's standing orders. These had been collated from various senior masters' standing orders and included no reference to the closing of the doors. Develin also told the police that the standing orders were devised to lessen the burden on the captain. He compared the need for reporting that the bow doors were closed with that of telling an engineer to lubricate the ship's engine before starting it. He said it was an issue 'fundamental to a deck officer's knowledge'. It was simply assumed.

'Things like saloons clean and tidy and tables laid and ready are not really comparable to the bow loading doors,' commented prosecuting counsel David Jeffreys. 'You can understand the master not wanting to be bombarded with a host of relatively unimportant items, but should that apply to such an important thing as bow doors?'

Numast has voiced concerns about standing orders in general. 'Most UK ship operating companies have long established Company's Standing Orders. The real problem is the fact that such orders are frequently used against masters and officers when such use is convenient to the company, but ignored by the company when it is commercially expedient to do so.'[10]

On the *Herald*, further confusion was caused by the fact that though the assistant bosun was nominally responsible for closing the doors, in practice he was not the only person responsible. It was common for others to close them. Indeed, Stanley said that on the majority of occasions someone had already closed them when he arrived at his post. The casual approach to such fundamental procedures was summed up by the deputy bosun at the Sheen inquiry. Asked who normally closed the doors, he replied: 'I might want a cup of tea and he [the assistant bosun] will shut the doors, or he might want a cup of tea and I will shut the doors. We are both capable of doing it.'

The system – such as it was – had already proved fallible. The *Herald*'s sister ship *Pride of Free Enterprise* was known to have set sail several times with its doors open, once when the assistant bosun fell asleep. It was also argued that the 'operating policy for the *Herald*, laid down by her senior master, was vague in comparison to the orders for her sister ship, the *Spirit of Free Enterprise*'. This was despite the fact that the *Herald*'s senior master had operated a positive reporting system when working on another of Townsend's ferries.

It is revealing to compare Townsend's system with the systems used by other operators. Sealink chairman James Sherwood said:

> The suggestion that ferries should have lights on the bridge to show whether the doors are open or closed is a red herring. Sealink British Ferries ships have always required a deck officer to be present on the car deck to supervise door closure, then to proceed to the bridge to report to the captain or to radio or telephone through the information. Bridge lights can malfunction.[11]

Responsible members of the company should be able to give clear and safe instructions

---

David Steel QC, counsel for the Secretary of State for Transport at the Sheen inquiry, concluded that negative reporting was

> a practice which manifestly is inherently dangerous. It is a practice which, whether or not suggested to him, the master had no business to operate.
>
> It involved many people over many years ... a failure to establish any system of supervising activity in terms of navigational safety and operations ... That in turn led to a failure to issue orders that the doors must be closed before departure and that an officer must check they are closed.
>
> It also led to the failure to require positive reporting of that fact to

the bridge and their failure to establish any form of monitoring that the system was properly operating.

When the company came to improve the orders after the disaster, the result was scarcely more satisfactory. It required an officer to make sure the assistant bosun was in position to close the doors rather than actually confirming the doors were shut. Sheen condemned them as 'unsatisfactory and ambiguous'. He called on senior Townsend staff to come and explain the procedures. 'There is a lack of clarity in these orders which should be dealt with. Responsible members of the company should be able to give clear and safe instructions,' he said. 'The whole system wants to be reviewed. The casualty occurred on 6 March and we are now eight days into this inquiry. I don't know why the company hasn't taken action already.'

Inadequacies in Townsend's safety procedures drew attention to the design flaws of ro-ro ferries which had been identified before Zeebrugge. On 1 January 1981, the shipping magazine *Fairplay* commented: 'The vast majority of ... casualties as investigated seemed to demonstrate that where the design was at fault it was the intolerance of the design to human error that was in the event responsible for the casualty rather than any inherent fault in the design itself.'

Stress on the ship's design and performance was increased because, in practice, calculations about the freight and passengers on board were often either ignored or inaccurate. Captain Lewry admitted that the ship's draught – its level in the water – was calculated on the estimated weight of the freight on board. In order to comply with maritime law these figures had to be recorded in the ship's log. Captain Lewry agreed that had the Department of Transport checked it would have noticed something wrong with the figures: they were not true readings.

There was equal vagueness about how many passengers the ship was carrying. This became evident when the company found it impossible to accurately calculate the number of casualties. It was reported at the Sheen inquiry that in September 1986 the master of the *Spirit of Free Enterprise* complained of overloading. It was, he said, a 'blatant and flagrant disregard for the system'. He had been told there were fewer than 1,300 people on his vessel. After a head count he found there were 1,550 – 150 more than the legal limit for both passengers and crew.

Seven other masters complained of overloading. In August 1986 the master of the *Pride of Free Enterprise* was told he had 1,228 passengers. A head count revealed there were 1,628. 'This total is way over the lifesaving capacity of the vessel,' he wrote to management on shore. 'The fine on the Master for this offence is £50,000 and probably confiscation of certificate. May I please know what steps the company intend to take to protect my career from mistakes of this nature.'[12]

As well as passengers, the *Herald* carried an extensive range of dangerous substances, materials people would perhaps be surprised to find on a cross-Channel ferry. It was estimated that there were 196 drums of toxic chemicals floating free in the car deck after the ship capsized. Two trucks aboard the ferry were carrying toxic chemicals, including 5 tonnes of toluene di-isocyanate; 11 tonnes of a cyanide solution; 20 tonnes of lead powder; several tonnes of tyrrolidine, methoxyethanol and toluene, plus 450 tonnes of diesel and lubricant oil. Illogically and dangerously, there are no special rules for toxic substances on ferries. Under the rules of the IMO, ferries are treated the same as any other craft. (They are also used as cargo vessels, though these have the same design frailties as passenger vessels.)

Had the passengers who sailed on that last fateful voyage known these things I suspect that most would have refused to set foot on the Herald

---

In addition to this potentially lethal cocktail of chemicals, calculations made since the disaster indicate that the vessel was 'very nearly over-loaded'. Indeed, the *Herald* was 250 to 270 tonnes heavier than it was supposed to be without cargo. The extra tonnage remains unexplained. No weight scales were used to measure the cargo. Instead, the tonnage was calculated by using the declarations of drivers. Experiments revealed that these were frequently false. An average ferry load of trucks was found to weigh 13 per cent more than the sum of drivers' declarations. Later Townsend took legal action against a number of lorry operators which it suspected had not declared the exact nature of their vehicles' loads when ferry space was booked or when vehicles were presented for embarkation. The company admitted that controlling what actually went on a ferry was beyond its capabilities. Little could be done to tighten up the procedure apart from examining every load and that would be impossible, it said.[13]

When it came to emergency procedures and equipment, the ferry also had a lengthy list of shortcomings. One survivor, Andrew Parker, when asked if there was anything he desperately needed during the ordeal, replied: 'Light, lifejackets and some information about what you should do in such an emergency.' The ship's evacuation plan assumed it would remain upright for 30 minutes after an incident. This patently ignored the suspicions of many in the industry and Townsend's own experience with the *European Gateway*. At the inquiry David Steel said the ship's evacuation plan was of 'limited value, if any'.

Charles Haddon-Cave, representing surviving passengers and bereaved relatives, described the problems faced by those trying to escape. Some passengers complained of difficulty in tying the straps on the lifejackets because their hands were numb with the cold. Many passengers were too weak to climb up the knotted ropes from the lifeboats. Internal glass partitions caused severe injury and made escape more difficult. The duty-free area was particularly hazardous with broken bottles flying around and fumes causing breathing difficulties. As if these difficulties weren't enough, most passengers were completely unprepared for an emergency. Haddon-Cave's conclusion was that 'had the passengers who sailed on that last fateful voyage known these things I suspect that most would have refused to set foot on the *Herald* that evening'.

I was shocked so little attention was paid to safety

After Zeebrugge a P&O advertisement trumpeted: 'Our captains and crew are highly qualified. Our pursers and cabin staff are trained to the most rigorous standards. So welcome to P&O European Ferries. Come aboard and feel the difference for yourself.' The difference was not always as pleasant as the advertisement proclaimed. Charles Wheeler, who served with the Department of Naval Equipment checking seamanship arrangements on naval vessels under construction in the 1970s, was appalled by what he saw on board the MV *Vortigern* (a vessel which P&O European Ferries chartered from Sealink for two months after Zeebrugge) during a crossing in thick fog to Boulogne. The former Royal Navy officer said: 'The crew must know the basics, and two of its members did not know where the liferafts were.'[14] He saw only 15 of the 43 rafts and found the rest in unmarked boxes. 'It would be very simple to provide every passenger with a slip of paper on arrival telling him simply where his emergency station is and how to find it. I was shocked that there was so little attention paid to safety,' said Wheeler.[15]

P&O European Ferries declined to comment, but Sealink confirmed that it had applied for the *Vortigern*'s safety certificate, which had been granted. 'That means the ship is safe,' Sealink said with confidence.[16]

Similar attitudes can be seen in the remarks of other ferry operators. David Langden, a director of Brittany Ferries, for example, has commented: 'Ferry companies are much safer than they are given credit for, and this will reflect well when the public starts considering travelling along a hole in the ground to Europe.'[17] Such pronouncements avoid the real issue by seeking to compare ferry safety, which has a record over a long period of time, with a form of cross-Channel transport which is, until 1993, hypothetical.

The Honourable Company of Master Mariners also remained confident of the safety and capabilities of ro-ros. 'British ferries are well managed, operated and manned,' it said in 1988. 'The cause of the loss of the *Herald* was exceptional. The human failures which precipitated the disaster should not happen again.' In response to concerns about ro-ros, Jim Buckley, deputy director-general of the GCBS, continued to exude confidence. 'We are proud and confident of the standards of safety for British ships. Ferry transport is a very safe form of travel,' he said.[18]

Despite such protestations, unsafe acts continued to take place after Zeebrugge. In October 1987, Dr James Cowley, surveyor-general of the Marine Directorate, stated that a number of reports had been received of ferries crossing harbours with bow or stern doors open. 'This is not a safe practice,' he commented.

The most dangerous part of the journey is driving to the port

---

Whether there have been improvements in ferry safety practices is still questioned. *Holiday Which?* research into ferry safety found that on one ferry almost half the passengers would be expected to escape down a 60-foot rope ladder.[19] A survey on board a ferry found that only 59 per cent of passengers could identify the muster sign correctly. Drawing on the risk analysis undertaken by Lloyd's Register, the report claimed ferry travel was one of the most dangerous forms of public transport with one collision expected every year, a fire every two to three years and a capsize every five years. As there would not be enough lifeboat space if the deck were cut off by fire or the ship listed, the report called for enough lifeboats to enable passengers to be evacuated from either side of the ship.

The researchers found that evacuation plans had failed to respond to the experiences of the *Herald* and *European Gateway*. (Survivors from the *European Gateway* alleged afterwards that there was a lack of lifejackets and the lifeboats could not be used.) They were told by the captain of one modern ferry that the minimum time for evacuation would be one to two hours. On the newest ferry they calculated an evacuation time of 43.5 minutes – this assumes an orderly evacuation with no bad weather, no rough water and no panic. None of this breaches regulations. While companies have to show that there is enough lifesaving equipment for all on board and that it works, they do not have to prove that they can safely evacuate a ship within 30 minutes in order to be granted a certificate to carry passengers.

The *Holiday Which?* report called for an independent public transport safety commission to back and help fund new safety research and to oversee standards. In response one ferry operator said: 'They under-estimate all the work that has taken place since Zeebrugge and some of their figures are very dodgy. The most dangerous part of the journey is driving to the port.' The Passenger Shipping Association, representing most of the large operators, said all safety regulations were met. P&O claimed: 'We are ahead of the international standards. If the standards have to be changed, that is up to the Department of Transport.'[20]

Lessons on evacuation could have been learned far earlier. In a test evacuation, shortly before Zeebrugge, the Royal National Lifeboat Institution used one hundred marines as passengers. Even they had difficulty escaping from a ferry. In 1979 a Danish ferry, the *Winston Churchill*, had to be evacuated en route from Gothenburg to Newcastle. It took four helicopters and seven boats five hours to rescue all 660 people on board.

After the Zeebrugge disaster, *Lloyd's List* revealed that the *Herald*'s insurers were 'to pay little more than half the £25 million insured value of the vessel'.[21] The reasons, it said, were that the ship was scrapped rather than repaired. This knocked £5 million off the total insurance sum. There was, however, a second reduction – 35 per cent of the remaining £20 million. This was because the vessel, according to the insurers, 'sailed in an unseaworthy condition'. *Lloyd's List* concluded: 'The settlement, which P&O had hoped to keep secret, indicates considerable doubt about the validity of P&O's claim.' How a ship can be, or be allowed to be, 65 per cent seaworthy was left unexplained by both P&O and the insurers.

References

1. *The Daily Telegraph*, 9 April 1987.
2. Department of Transport Marine Directorate, HMSO, 1991.
3. BBC Radio 4, *Shock Waves*, part 2, 18 April 1991.
4. Merchant Shipping Notice No. M1188, 'Good ship management', Department of Transport, July 1986.
5. *The Sunday Times*, 15 April 1990.
6. BBC *World at One*, 9 October 1987.
7. *Management Today*, July 1990.
8. BBC Radio 4, *Shock Waves*, part 3, 25 April 1991.
9. *The Safety of Ro-Ro Passenger Ferries*, J. R. Spouge, RINA, 1988.
10. Quoted by Lord Underhill, House of Lords, 14 December 1987.
11. *The Times*, 23 May 1987.
12. Sheen report, para. 17.17.
13. *Motor Transport*, 30 April 1987.
14. Letter in *The Daily Telegraph*, 21 April 1987.
15. *The Daily Telegraph*, 21 April 1987.
16. Ibid.
17. *The Sunday Times*, 5 April 1990.
18. *The Times*, 24 March 1989.
19. *Holiday Which?*, September 1990.
20. *The Daily Telegraph*, 7 September 1990.
21. *Lloyd's List International*, 11 February 1988.

CHAPTER FIVE

PEOPLE AT WORK

'Herald has had a raw deal'
– senior master of the *Herald.*

'If I was driving a jumbo jet, which carried less people,
I would be put in prison'
– P&O second officer.

The Department of Transport's Marine Directorate commented as follows in its 1991 report, *The Human Element in Shipping Casualties*:

> When everything else has been looked at and tried – newer designs, better technical aids, the increase in ever more sophisticated regulations and enforcement systems at every level – one thing remains about which there is, almost universally, agreement as to the underlying cause of casualties – the human factor.
>
> In transport, people – how they are treated and motivated, as well as the systems and procedures they work under – are the key to safety. If they are vigilant, constantly made aware of safety issues, well trained, competent, well managed and working within safe systems, the opportunity for human error is radically reduced. If one of these elements is not in place, a constant risk is run.

---

*Shipping is the only mode of transport
which allows working hours to be unregulated*

The design of ro-ro vessels brought with it the implicit risk of human error. It was a risk repeatedly identified by researchers and actually experienced by many ferry companies across the world – including Townsend Thoresen. In these circumstances it was vital that Townsend's personnel were highly trained, well organised and motivated. But, in reality, the failure of safety procedures and standing orders were just two deficiencies resulting from the way Townsend treated its personnel.

The fact that the assistant bosun regularly slept during his time on the ship drew attention to the hours actually worked by officers and crew. Townsend officers worked 12 hours on board ship and not fewer than 24 hours off. In contrast, each crew member was on board ship for 24 hours and then had 48 hours ashore. On the *Herald* three crews intersected five different sets of officers. This arrangement meant that stable working relationships were unlikely to be developed. Soon after Zeebrugge, Sealink chairman James Sherwood commented:

> I believe a contributory factor to the Zeebrugge disaster may be that officers and ratings have different duty rotations on a vessel. We at Sealink British Ferries are trying to stop this practice. If the same officers and ratings always work together as a crew we think discipline will improve and the possibility of misunderstanding over work procedures will be reduced.[1]

These hours and arrangements were not unusual. As Richard Goss of the Department of Maritime Studies at the University of Wales said:

> It is remarkable that there is no regulation of the hours to be worked by ships' officers and, especially, their captains. To bring a ship through the Western Approaches, up the English Channel and into, say London, Felixstowe or Rotterdam may take some days. The weather is often hazy and the traffic is always dense. It is remarkable that shipping is the only mode of transport in which British law allows working hours to be unregulated, whilst assuming that a ship's captain is always able to be alert when wanted.[2]

The situation on cross-Channel ferries is worsened by the fact that time pressures are intense, danger is always present and there are hundreds of passengers on board. Technological advances mean that the ratio of crew to passengers has grown ever smaller.

---

*Proper rest is fundamental to a
safe and efficient service*

The demands on seafarers are probably unique in British industry and undoubtedly unique in a business in which safety factors are particularly significant. Captain M. H. Collier, formerly chief marine superintendent of Sealink, says: 'Crews, particularly officers, should not only be competent, but temperamentally suited to the work imposed on them. Intense activity without respite for periods of up to 12 hours requires a certain temperament if the system is to run smoothly and efficiently.'[3]

For no apparent reason, the hours worked by mariners are less well monitored than those worked in other parts of the transport industry. While truck drivers have a tachograph ('the spy in the cab') recording their hours at the wheel and the flying time of pilots is carefully limited, mariners suffer no such restrictions. Efforts to regulate the working hours of mariners seem grounded in apathy. In 1979 the Department of Transport produced proposed work safety regulations covering the hours worked by merchant seamen. By the time of the Zeebrugge disaster, these had not been finalised.

'Proper rest is fundamental to a safe and efficient service for fast ferries. Neither safety nor service can be provided by tired people,' says Numast. Undoubtedly, 12-hour shifts are tiring. The situation is hardly helped by the taking of occasional naps. In the case of the *Herald*, the assistant bosun was a heavy sleeper. Usually when he planned to sleep he left his boots outside his cabin; then when he was needed it would be evident that he would have to be woken up. The system of work relied on a casual and dangerous arrangement.

Even in 1991, the issue of working hours remains unresolved. The government continues to consult companies and unions on draft regulations to set fixed hours of work and rest for seamen. At the 1991 Numast conference, a P&O second officer said that he had worked a 77-hour week on nightshifts on the Dover–Zeebrugge service. 'If I was driving a jumbo jet, which carries less people, I would be put in prison,' he admitted.

The government's excuse for this lack of regulation is curious. In December 1987, Lord Brabazon, Minister for Aviation and Shipping, admitted in the House of Lords: 'There is no reliable medical method of determining whether a person is fatigued'. Lord Underhill replied: 'I find it hard to appreciate that it is difficult to get a definition of fatigue in the light of the fact that the department has been considering the matter for something like seven or eight years.'

Perhaps the clearest sign of fatigue is that tired people make mistakes. The Hidden report into the Clapham rail disaster highlighted tiredness as a significant factor in the mistakes that were made. A total of 28 per cent of British Rail's workforce had worked seven days a week for the 13 weeks before the accident and 34 per cent had worked 13 days out of the previous 14. Of the employee who made the critical error, the report said, 'constant repetition of weekend work ... had blunted his working edge'. Amazingly, the statistics available to senior BR engineers failed to tell them that the technicians were working such long hours.

A serious loss of continuity

The exhausting hours worked by seafarers were supplemented on the *Herald* by a climate of insecurity. There was a basic lack of continuity. It is not an isolated instance. 'Well organised airlines may possess a considerable esprit de corps, and I think that civil aviation has many of them. It is a long time since the same could be said of shipping,' says Richard Goss of the University of Wales. Manning levels on the *Herald* were complicated by the fact that it alternated between the Zeebrugge run and other, shorter ferry routes, such as Dover–Calais. Temporary officers were added and subtracted according to the route taken. Additionally, the *Herald* was used as a training vessel for new officers. This simply added to the rotation of officers.

At $4\frac{1}{2}$ hours, the Zeebrugge route was longer than the other routes the *Herald* operated on. In response, Townsend had reduced the number of officers from four to three (a master and two deck officers). It argued that the longer sailing time from Dover to Zeebrugge gave them more time to relax. This provoked complaints about manning levels. It was reported at the Sheen inquiry that Captain Kirby, the senior master, wrote an internal memo at the end of 1986 to the chief superintendent. 'The existing system of deck officer manning ... is unsatisfactory,' said Kirby.

> When the *Herald* took up the Zeebrugge service our deck officers were reduced from the usual complement of 15 to 10. The surplus five were distributed around the fleet. On the *Herald*'s return to the Calais service, instead of our own officers returning to the ship, we were and are being manned by officers from whatever ship is at refit.
>
> Due to this system, together with trainee master moves, *Herald* will have had a total of 30 different deck officers on the books during the period 29 September 1986 to 5 January 1987. This makes continuity of jobs which have to be the particular responsibility of individual officers very difficult ... I suspect that the standards of maintenance and checks are falling back and there is no doubt that the bosuns and deck crews are confused by the number of different

officers they have to work under ... I believe that *Herald* has had a raw deal this winter.

The complaint had no effect and a couple of months later Kirby was restating his case in another memo:

Herald badly needs a permanent complement of good deck officers ... The result has been a serious loss of continuity. Shipboard maintenance, safety gear checks, crew training and the overall smooth running of the vessel have all suffered ... This memo is a plea that you do not take any further 'Permanent?' (Joke!) deck officers from *Herald* and that the gaps be filled with first-class officers. Thereafter, I hope that the ship will be allowed a long period of officer stability.

Clearly the safe and efficient operation of a ship relies on teamwork and settled working relationships. These were not in place on the *Herald*. Before a 'long period of officer stability' could be introduced, the ship was on its way to a scrapyard in Taiwan.

Confusion was heightened by the fact that standing orders were not common across the Townsend fleet. Procedures on one ship could differ from those on others, and often did.

P&O, in a statement in 1988, made it clear where the responsibility for organising the crew lay. 'The internal organisation of the ship is a matter for the discretion of the master. He follows the standard contingency plan for his vessel which allows sufficient flexibility for back up with qualified personnel for any eventuality.'[4] Despite the rapid turnover of officers and lengthy hours, the Sheen report believed there was 'no reason why the *Herald* could not have been safely and efficiently operated on the Dover–Zeebrugge run ... if proper thought had been given to the organisation of their duties'.

Working hours have remained a bone of contention. After Zeebrugge more stringent tests on loading were introduced, but no extra personnel were brought in. One report, later in 1987, claimed that the *Spirit of Free Enterprise* put to sea with up to six of the agreed crew of 17 deck ratings absent because of leave or sickness. Later in 1987 P&O denied union claims that it was going to make eight hundred people redundant. 'In some cases, crew members work fewer than 80 days a year for a full year's pay,' P&O said in a statement. 'We want to achieve a minimum working year which would still allow 218 days off duty. We would like to have a ratio of two and a half crews per ship.'[5] At the time there were at least 3.6 crews per ship.

'I find it hard to believe that any reduction will increase safety,' commented Commodore Gordon Greenfield, president of the Nautical Institute and one of the assessors at the Sheen inquiry.

P&O proposed officers should work on the vessel for a minimum of 72 hours and a maximum of 136. This allowed six hours' sleep per day and two hours for meals. The company was within its rights to require such extraordinary commitment as there are no statutory limitations on hours of work for officers. It claimed that many of its Dover workforce had '243 days off' every year under the new terms of employment. This figure appeared generous but was arrived at by dividing the sum total of hours that crew members spent away from their place of work by 24, resulting in a figure expressed in days. Using these rules, someone working a conventional five-day working week of 9am to 5.30pm, without a lunch hour, and enjoying 20 days' holiday (including national holidays), has around 280 days off per annum. Those who take a regular lunch hour spend ten days a year at lunch.

---

*Crew are simply unable to discharge
their duties and responsibilities*

The arguments continued to rage long after. In 1988 the safety officer on P&O's *European Clearway* left the company. 'My feeling is that current working conditions and in particular the hours which crew are expected to work without proper rest periods mean that the crew are simply unable to discharge their duties and responsibilities properly in order to ensure the safe carriage of passengers,' he told the *Daily Mail*.

The magazine *Private Eye* continued to wage a campaign against P&O's personnel policies. In 1991 it claimed:

> Not everyone who works for P&O is entirely delighted with the agreement employees have been asked to sign about working conditions on board the company's ferries. Its aim is simple – more work done by fewer employees – and two clauses have caused particular offence. The first obliges a crew member to work his relief's tour of duty if the relief does not turn up because of sickness;

the second ... requires all employees to give management the right to inspect their medical records.[6]

Safety training, and P&O's attitude to it, was again raised in August 1991 when a newspaper revealed that P&O crew members actually had to *pay* for basic safety training. A recruitment agency used by the company charged people £51 for basic sea-survival and fire-fighting lessons. The agency claimed it was a device to increase 'worker loyalty'. One of the recruits recalled:

> I was sent to a college and given pages of information on things like where lifeboats are kept on a ferry, and how to evacuate in an emergency. But you don't get a chance to practise any of this on a ship. When I worked on a ferry for the first time it was up to me to find out where the evacuation points and passengers' lifejackets were.

P&O, in response, said it knew nothing of the arrangement and immediately ordered it to stop.[7]

Abject abdication of responsibility

While the question of working hours and manning levels was clearly a matter of great contention, at the time of the Zeebrugge disaster other personnel matters remained imprecisely defined or ignored. Job descriptions – the very meat and drink of any personnel policy – were vague or non-existent. In a meeting of senior masters and management before Zeebrugge, a request was made to provide job descriptions for ship's officers. Marine superintendent Jeffrey Develin said that, although he was still considering writing definitions of these different roles, he felt 'it was more preferable not to define the roles but to allow them to evolve'. Sheen described this as 'an abject abdication of responsibility. It demonstrates an inability or unwillingness to give clear orders. Clear instructions are the foundation of a safe system of operation.' The consequence, he said, was simple: 'The directors did not have any proper comprehension of what their duties were.'

There were also worrying signs of weak, if not apathetic, personnel management. Alcohol, for example, was freely drunk by crew when on duty – they were even given discounts. Astonishingly, alcohol bought at preferential rates on board ship *had* to be consumed on board. Four months after Zeebrugge, the company wrote to the unions proposing greater restrictions on drinking on board. The move, it explained, was prompted by 'safety and public image considerations ... part of a safety review covering all aspects of sailing procedure following the inquiry into the Zeebrugge accident'. In a disturbing admission, the company said: 'Alcohol consumption is in excess of what could be considered acceptable. We wish to have a situation where a minimum amount of alcohol is consumed aboard by seafarers and seek your support to achieve this.'[8]

On one occasion in 1989, the second officer on the *Pride of Canterbury* drove to his ship after he had been drinking and just 11 days after being banned from driving. When stopped by police with twice the legal limit of alcohol he said, 'The ship can't sail without me.' His solicitor said in his defence: 'P&O were very short-staffed and the dire necessity to be on that ship became the over-riding factor in his mind.' He was not, of course, in breach of any maritime rules.

---

*Work records didn't come into it
when we were pulling bodies out of the sea*

While P&O's advertising continued to laud the training and professionalism of its crews, its treatment of survivors from the crew of the *Herald* earned few plaudits. In October 1987 a report that surviving crewmen and their families had been offered a free cruise on the luxury liner *Canberra* appeared on the front page of the *Daily Star* under the headline 'Sick!' There were also claims that many survivors had had the three weeks immediately following the disaster 'docked' from their annual leave and that the father of one victim had not been paid for the fortnight he took off for bereavement. P&O responded to such reports by claiming that 'all leave arrangements were agreed with the union, and all survivors have received ex-gratia payments'.[9] There were accusations that surviving crew members with 'poor work records' had had their compensation cut by P&O. One of those accusations came from stewardess Gail Cook, who had shepherded survivors to safety despite a broken collarbone. She said after being offered £28,900 compensation by the company:

> Work records didn't come into it when we were pulling bodies out
> of the sea that freezing cold night. I don't know anyone on the ship

that night who hasn't got some blemish against them. But that had nothing to do with how we performed saving passengers. We weren't even given the chance to argue our case and say whether we thought the company had their facts right.

Steward John Butler spent six hours plucking dying passengers from the sea and was offered £25,800.

We are just groping along

Front-page stories in the *Daily Mirror* produced a hasty about-turn by P&O.[10] A few days later it announced: 'We've instructed the insurers to eliminate any adverse factors relating to work records that could affect survivors' settlements.' 'It's a pity it took all this publicity to bring the company to its senses,' said MP Michael Meacher.

The *Herald*'s captain, David Lewry, received the equivalent of a year's pay by way of compensation. P&O also dropped disciplinary charges against him when he resigned. It is believed that the arrangement included a binding clause preventing him speaking about the capsize of the ferry and the company's safety system.[11]

Seven months after Zeebrugge, an investigation by the Press Association (PA) into P&O's treatment of the crew found only four then had jobs at sea. The rest were faced with psychological and financial problems. 'Many of the 19 *Herald* crew who have left the company being considered unfit to go back to sea, cannot get medical severance payments because of shipping industry bureaucracy. They were classed as seasonal workers rather than registered seafarers, although some had been with Townsend for five years,' the PA reported.

'We don't know what is going to happen. We know the moment we take medical severance, that is the end of our wages – then the dole starts. We are just groping along,' said *Herald* bosun Terry Ayling.

'The company has treated employees abominably,' said a Dover solicitor; while David Shaw, Conservative MP for Dover, described it as 'a ludicrous and stupid situation'. Peter Ford, chairman of P&O European Ferries, responded:

We are not pretending there were never any mistakes. Of course there were, but there was never any malicious intention to screw these guys down. We have been trying to deal with thousands of problems arising from the catastrophe. A lot of the managers have been close to breaking-point.

The management have borne as much strain, in my opinion, as many of the crew members. To some degree, almost everyone in the company needs counselling.[12]

References

1. *The Times*, 23 May 1987.
2. 'Legislation, regulation and enforcement: shipping', Richard Goss, paper presented at Royal Aeronautical Society/RINA Conference on Safety at Sea and in the Air: Taking Stock Together, 1990.
3. 'The Influence of Operational Procedures on Ro-Ro Safety', M. H. Collier, paper presented at Kummerman International Conference on Ro-Ro Safety and Stability, 1987.
4. P&O press release, 3 May 1988.
5. Ibid.
6. *Private Eye*, 1 March 1991.
7. *Sunday Mirror*, 4 August 1991.
8. *The Daily Telegraph*, 3 July 1987.
9. *Daily Mirror*, 23 August 1988.
10. *Daily Mirror*, 24 and 27 August 1988.
11. *Evening Standard*, 1 February 1988.
12. *Guardian*, 23 December 1987.

CHAPTER SIX

SHEEN AND THE DISEASE OF SLOPPINESS

'In the circumstances Townsend Car Ferries accepts that this
casualty was caused by its own faults and the faults of its employees.
It is right … that the company should take the responsibility.'
– Townsend's counsel at the Sheen inquiry.

'… too much heed has been paid to the need to avoid damaging
commercial operation'
– Marshall Meek of RINA.

In the weeks following the Zeebrugge disaster the weight of blame hung
uneasily in the air as the truth of what happened slowly emerged. The
public inquiry, when it opened on Monday 27 April, provided a shift in
emphasis. The burden of blame spread from the very first day. Though the
actions of individual crew members were brought into question, the ferry
company's management and organisation came under intense scrutiny.

As the inquiry opened in front of Justice Sheen (a former Royal Navy
captain) and four assessors, the *Herald* was being refloated and more
bodies were being recovered. There was still confusion over the number
of missing persons. Commenting on the expectations of the public, *The
Times* said that Sheen would 'have the awful responsibility of knowing
that if he gets the safety factors wrong, the next disaster could be on the
scale of the *Titanic*'.[1]

Despite the fact that Mark Stanley had said that he left the doors open,
P&O managers still professed to believe in the idea that the *Herald* had
struck something in the water. P&O chairman Sir Jeffrey Sterling remained confident that the company was not to blame. 'I would be very
surprised if [the disaster] proves to be other than avoidable human error,'
he said before the inquiry began.[2] But on the first day, David Steel QC,

71

counsel for the Secretary of State for Transport, said: 'The disease of sloppy system and sloppy practice infected not just those on board the ship, but infected well into the body corporate of Townsend Thoresen.'

It involves many people over many years

It was a theme developed throughout the inquiry. 'The fault of management was a fault which could be found all the way from junior superintendents in the marine department through to the board of directors. It is a failure to ensure that there was a proper system of management at all,' said Steel in a vigorous critique of the way the business was run. He went on:

Its particular impact was a failure to establish any system of supervising activity in terms of navigational safety and operations. That in turn led to a failure to issue orders that the doors must be closed before departure and that an officer must check they are closed.

It also led to the failure to require positive reporting of that fact to the bridge and their failure to establish any form of monitoring that the system was properly operating ... it involves many people over many years.

The response from the company seemed to indicate a change of attitude, an acceptance of its responsibility. 'There was no reason why those on board, the master or the senior master, should not have had a system which ensured that the loading officer checked that the doors were closed,' said its counsel.

It is accepted by Townsend Thoresen that their instructions could and should have contained an explicit instruction [on bow doors]. In the circumstances Townsend Car Ferries accepts that this casualty was caused by its own faults and the faults of its employees. It is right in our submission that the company should take the responsibility.

Even so, the company still maintained that the reason the bow doors were left open was 'avoidable human error'.

For his part, Captain Lewry said: 'I feel whichever master had been on that day the same thing would have happened.' Nevertheless, his counsel admitted: 'He fully accepts with hindsight that it was an inadequate system that he took over.'

At the inquiry, the company was represented by a series of managers and directors. Their performance, both as managers and as witnesses, was severely criticised by Sheen. *The Times* later called it 'unpleasant slipperiness'. Of technical director Wallace Ayers, Sheen made the withering condemnation:

Mr Ayers may be a competent naval architect, but the Court formed the view that he did not carry out his managerial duties, whatever they may have been. Mr Ayers was asked whether each director of Townsend Car Ferries was given a specific area of responsibility. His answer was 'No, there were no written guidelines for any director'. When he was asked how each director knew what his responsibilities were, his answer was 'It was more a question of duplication as a result of not knowing than missing gaps. We were a team who had grown together'. The amorphous phrasing of that answer is typical of much of the evidence of Mr Ayers. He appeared to be incapable of expressing his thoughts with clarity.

Flippant, facetious and fatuous

Marine superintendent Jeffrey Develin fared little better. During questioning he admitted that he had misled the inquiry about when he had first heard a proposal to fit warning lights on ferry bridges. Initially, he claimed that 7 March, the day after the disaster, was the first time the idea had occurred to him. Develin subsequently broke down, admitting his 'answer was muddled'. It was also revealed that he discounted warnings from one of the company's senior masters about potential dangers because he thought the captains were exaggerating. Sheen described Develin's responses to the legitimate concerns of the masters as 'flippant, facetious and fatuous'. The new orders drawn up by Develin shortly after the disaster were also condemned by Sheen.

After 29 days of listening to evidence in the Assembly Hall of the administrative headquarters of the Church of England, the court delivered its findings on 24 July. As a result Captain Lewry lost his master's certificate for a year and Leslie Sabel lost his for two, in spite of which the two men issued a joint statement saying the report was 'fair and well-balanced'. More importantly, Sheen spread the blame far wider than those directly charged with closing the ship's doors. 'Cardinal faults lay higher up in the company,' he said. Guilt lay with 'all concerned in management. From top to bottom, the body corporate was infected with the disease of sloppiness.'

The findings of the inquiry encouraged many to call for sanctions against the company. Conservative MP Terry Dicks said: 'The people of this country want to see the management of Townsend punished. And I think the sooner the company is closed down the better.' Another MP said: 'The management is obviously rotten to the core and the people of this country expect tough action'; while Labour's Brian Sedgemore denounced P&O as 'merchants of death'. The *Daily Express* called the report 'a devastating indictment'.

Appraising the report, Peter Ford, chairman of P&O European Ferries, simply commented: 'The judge has made some tough and pungent comments about management of the company and the individuals involved.'[3]

Too much heed has been paid to the need to avoid damaging commercial operation

---

While Sheen's report uncovered many of the disturbing aspects of the *Herald* capsize, other fundamental issues were given less prominence. The report, for example, makes little reference to the loss of the *European Gateway*, the event which should have alerted all ferry operators to the potential danger of a ro-ro ferry capsizing or sinking rapidly. Indeed, the fundamental issues of ro-ro vulnerability were consigned to the outer reaches of the report under the heading 'Future design issues'. Sheen said it was 'not the function of this court to redesign the entire ferry fleet'.

'One is left with the feeling that too much heed has been paid to the need to avoid damaging commercial operation,' concluded the RINA's Marshall Meek. David Tench, legal officer of the Consumers' Association, expressed similar feelings: 'The report ... leads to one inescapable conclusion. When it comes to a conflict between the safety of passengers on the high seas and the commercial interests of the shipping industry, the commercial interests seem to win every time.'

In such an inquisitorial – rather than adversarial – inquiry, it is rare for blame to be attached strongly to any one party. In this case, however,

Townsend received the full brunt of Sheen's limited powers under the 1970 Merchant Shipping Act. 'There is,' he said, 'no other way in which this court can mark its feelings about the conduct of Townsend Car Ferries other than by an order that they should pay a substantial part of the costs of this investigation.' The company was ordered to pay £350,000, with an additional £50,000 to the NUS, which represented surviving crew and relatives of the crew who died. In response, Townsend argued that much of the inquiry had dealt with matters of public interest which were not strictly to do with the company. 'No time was wasted,' responded Sheen with forceful simplicity.

References

1. *The Times*, 3 April 1987.
2. *The Times*, 24 April 1987.
3. *Daily Express*, 25 July 1987.

CHAPTER SEVEN

INTERNAL COMMUNICATIONS

'If the sensible suggestion that indicator lights be installed
had received ... the serious consideration which it
deserved ... this disaster might well
have been prevented'
– Sheen report.

'Communications between the ship and shore were inadequate'
– counsel in the Central Criminal Court.

The lack of an efficient communications system – both on board ship and ashore – was a crucial element in the Zeebrugge disaster. On board ship the communications failure was highlighted by the lack of positive reporting. A simple act of communication – the assistant bosun having to report 'bow doors closed' on the telephone link with the bridge – would have prevented the disaster. The inadequacy of the ship's standing orders and reporting systems was symptomatic of a wider inability to communicate effectively. The impression given at the public inquiry was of managers existing in their own shore-bound world, unwilling or unable to understand or even listen to the concerns of the masters.

It is not my responsibility

Business guru J. K. Galbraith has observed: 'To the adherents of the institutional truth there is nothing more inconvenient, nothing that so contributes to discomfort, than open, persistent, articulate assertion of what is real.' Too often, the institutional truth – assuming that things are as you want them to be – takes precedence over what actually happens.

Poor, or non-existent, communications channels have played a part in many other disasters. The *Titanic* received four warnings of ice floes on its route. The last warning, of ice directly in its way, never reached the captain. At the inquiry into the Aberfan coal-tip disaster, which killed 144 children and adults in 1966, it was concluded that 'it was a matter not of wickedness but of ignorance, ineptitude and a failure in communications'. Warnings had been ignored. In June 1972 a British European Airways Trident crashed killing all 118 passengers. The public inquiry suggested that, if more attention had been paid to an earlier reported event, the crew might have been better prepared to deal with the emergency. Similarly, the Fennell report into the 1988 King's Cross disaster said that London Underground's failure to implement proposals resulting from earlier fires had contributed to the disaster.

The failure of communications has broad implications. If communications systems don't work, individuals cannot learn from the experience of others. If their protestations are ignored, they will retreat into a self-contained world. They may follow regulations and orders to the letter but no more.

The potential end-result is demonstrated by the case of the ferry *Scandinavian Star*. When a fire broke out on board this ship in 1990 it was reported to the staff captain. He did not know the extent of the fire or its type; such information was simply not reported to him and he did not seek to find out. 'It is not my responsibility,' he said by way of explanation. He automatically assumed that the fuel supply to the engine room had been cut off. In fact, it was feeding the fire.[1]

The 1988 Clapham rail crash inquiry revealed similar attitudes and assumptions within British Rail. When BR managers introduced a new instruction on wiring they gave no explanation or training. 'They confined themselves to a false belief that the instruction was being implemented in spirit. Such a belief had about it little more than a pious hope and had nothing to do with good management,' said Sir Anthony Hidden's report into the disaster. The coroner's inquest on the Clapham victims revealed that crucial testing instructions had not been given to key staff. Managers had played 'pass the parcel' with the manual issued six months before the crash. They believed that once an instruction was in place it lived a life of its own, implemented and obeyed blindly without managerial interference. Effective communication of what the instructions entailed was assumed.

Even companies with the best of intentions often fall down in communicating them. At the 1989 European Business Ethics Network conference, it was reported that a quarter of European companies with ethical codes failed to circulate them either to external interest groups or to all employees.

*It treated the worries of its masters
with frivolous contempt*

In Townsend's case, the worries of its masters -- trained professionals –
were treated with frivolous contempt. In May 1985 the company's marine
department received a proposal that bow door indicator lights should be
installed so that masters would know if the doors were safely closed. The
suggestion came from Captain Bob Blowers of the *Herald*'s sister ship,
Pride of Free Enterprise. His request followed an occasion when his ship
had taken out to sea with the bow doors open after the assistant bosun fell
asleep – exactly what was to happen to the *Herald of Free Enterprise*.
Blowers's memo was sent to Jeffrey Develin and circulated in his department. The reaction of Develin and his colleagues was called 'quite
shocking' by Sheen. Deputy chief superintendent John Alcindor said:
'Do they need an indicator to tell them whether the deck storekeeper
[assistant bosun] is awake and sober ... my goodness!' Superintendent
for the *Herald* class Ron Ellison responded: 'Assume the guy who shuts
the doors tells them there's a problem.' Others were equally casual. 'Nice
– but don't we already pay someone?' said one manager. Superintendent
David Hamilton simply remarked: 'Nice'.

Between June 1985 and October 1986 three ferry masters wrote to ask
for warning lights. 'If the sensible suggestion that indicator lights be
installed had received, in 1985, the serious consideration which it deserved, it is at least possible that they would have been fitted in the early
months of 1986 and this disaster might well have been prevented,' said
Sheen. After the disaster the indicator lights were fitted at a cost of less
than £500 per ship.

*Shore management clearly took little notice of what
it was told by the masters*

Communications between masters were similarly flawed. Lewry, for
example, did not know that the *Herald*'s sister ship had sailed with its
bow doors open four times. 'If I had known, I would have immediately
instigated positive reporting on the bridge and then requested light indicators,' he said. This ignorance of what was happening elsewhere in the

fleet actually helped when it came to defending P&O European Ferries against corporate manslaughter. How could Lewry have known there was an obvious risk if he had never received the reports from other vessels?

Requests and criticism provoked defensiveness and inaction. 'Develin was inclined to blame any shortcomings in the system on the senior masters,' observed Sheen. Other managers were equally defensive on other matters. When Tony Young, the port operations director, received a memo from a captain complaining that on four occasions his vessel had carried more passengers than the number officially recorded, he thought 'it was quite an unfair criticism to make of the shore staff'.

Captain John Martin, one of the company's senior masters, received much the same response when he warned Develin of potential dangers involving the *Herald* and its sister ships on the Zeebrugge run. Martin pointed out that with the ship trimmed to the head, a wave would come three-quarters of the way up the bow doors. Develin said he 'thought it was an exaggeration'. Lewry also wrote six months before the disaster warning of the dangers of filling the ship's bow ballast tanks in order to load at Zeebrugge. These requests and entreaties were rebuffed.

Shore management clearly took very little notice of what it was told by the masters. There was a period of two and a half years during which there was no formal meeting between management and senior masters. This silence meant that the instructions issued by Captain Kirby and his predecessors for the *Herald* were never reviewed by shore staff. The situation was not helped by the apparent antipathy between those with engineering backgrounds, who were generally shore bound, and those with nautical training and experience.

If he had been unhappy …
he would have come and banged my desk

Within the company, methods of communication had fallen into disrepair or simple disuse. Since memos written by masters were disregarded, there was little motivation for them to provide honest and practical criticism of the way the company, its ships and operations worked. Managers on shore took the attitude that if something was important, a master would do something more than write a mere memo. One of many examples was Develin's reaction to a memo from Captain Martin in 1983. 'Initially I was not happy. When I studied it further, I decided that it was an operational difficulty report and Captain Martin was acquainting me of it,' recalled Develin. He said at the inquiry: 'I think if he had been unhappy with the problem he would have come and banged my desk.'

All of this highlights two complementary areas of responsibility. Managers have a responsibility to ensure there are lines of communication so that subordinates can voice legitimate concerns about working practices. Subordinates must have a responsibility to continue to voice their concerns and make sure action is taken if they believe these concerns are serious enough. This may involve what is now called 'whistle blowing'. A classic example in a different field is the experience of the 'O' ring seal expert employed by a NASA supplier, Morton Thiokol. When he tried unsuccessfully to stop the launch of the space shuttle *Challenger* in 1986 because he had serious reservations about the seal, he was overruled by top management. *Challenger* exploded shortly after take-off. The man was chastised by his chief executive and demoted, and eventually left the company, despite being praised by a national inquiry for his stand.

P&O deckhand Eddie Ottley received comparable treatment. He filled in a health and safety complaint form when the P&O ferry *Free Enterprise VII* sailed with its bow doors open nine months after Zeebrugge. 'All moorings were let go before bow doors were closed. Again it seems that time comes before safety due to late sailing,' he wrote immediately after the incident. Two days later he was interviewed by two P&O captains and told: 'This is a bit heavy isn't it?' The complaint was not raised at the ship's next safety committee meeting. Ottley claims that he was later sacked.[2]

Reference

1. *Seaways* (Journal of the Nautical Institute), March 1990.
2. *Daily Mirror*, 13 May 1988.

CHAPTER EIGHT

TALKING TO THE WORLD

'In a business environment … managers have to make decisions
about right actions from an ethical as well as technical point of view'
– Jon White of Cranfield School of Management.

'If you tell the truth, sooner or later you'll be found out'
– Oscar Wilde.

The way a company responds to a disaster – whether it be a tragic accident
or a dramatic financial reversal – is increasingly regarded as being an
accurate barometer of the kind of organisation it is. 'In a business
environment where consumers and employees are increasingly aware of
moral issues, managers have to make decisions about right actions from
an ethical as well as technical point of view,' says Jon White of Cranfield
School of Management. 'Otherwise, when a crisis occurs the response
tends to be a knee-jerk reaction rather than one which is seen to be rooted
in that company's moral principles about consumers, the environment or
the welfare of its employees.'[1]

A 1991 report, *The Power of the Open Company*, by communications
management consultancy Smythe Dorwood Lambert, surveyed 46 chief
executives of leading British companies including British Rail, British
Gas and BTR. 'Attention to reputation, where image matches reality, is
now a commercial imperative,' it concluded, and predicted that advertising and design would be supplanted in importance by public relations.
Crises and disasters provide the ultimate test of public relations as in their
aftermath the world listens more intently than ever before to the people
who represent individual companies.

When a British Midland plane crashed on the M1 with 47 deaths in
1989, British Midland chairman Sir Michael Bishop quickly emerged as a
credible, well-informed manager, clearly concerned to do the utmost for
those who had suffered. In a crisis his performance was an exemplary
example of calmness and honesty. It appeared to be 'rooted in the
company's moral principles'.

Others fare less well. After a fire at the Cairo Sheraton Hotel in which 17 were killed, a hotel spokesman gave the impression that out of eight hundred guests, 17 deaths was quite a good result under the circumstances.

A lack of clarity can be equally damning. After the fire on the *Scandinavian Star* in April 1990, the managing director of the parent company contradicted the impressions of survivors and refused to comment on whether the alarms worked properly or whether the crew was poorly rehearsed in the fire drill.

For P&O and the ferry operator it had taken over six weeks before the capsize, Zeebrugge was much more than a human disaster. Their reaction to it and the way they managed that reaction were symptomatic of the failings identified by Justice Sheen.

A lack of credibility was evident from the very start. As news came in on the night of the disaster, P&O's press office was poorly informed about events – admittedly confused – in Zeebrugge. The first television reports said the ship had 'apparently hit a seawall'. Later, it was said that the *Herald* capsized after its bow doors burst open on impact. At the press office, only two people were on hand to deal with enquiries. From a public relations point of view, they compounded that error by allowing a film crew into the office to record their confusion.

The reaction of Occidental employees to the *Piper Alpha* disaster provides a pointed contrast. Nearly 30 of its staff arrived at an emergency press room in London at midnight on the day of the disaster, while a hundred arrived at its Aberdeen office. From then on, the offices were manned around the clock until being wound down a month after the disaster. Regrettably, Occidental went on to spoil that early record with its insensitive treatment of bereaved relatives.

We are in the business of reassuring people

A few days after the Zeebrugge capsize (or 'accident' as P&O referred to it), Sterling wrote to all the company's employees, giving the casualty figures which were to prove so inaccurate and ending with the observation: 'It is surely a bitter irony that such a tragedy has taken place in one of the Group's proudest years.' Townsend's calculations bemused those still at the scene. A senior official advising the Belgian inquiry team said: 'We know that the figure of 132 people missing is nearly twice the number the ferry's owners are quoting, but we must insist that ours is the true figure ... Why Townsend still persists in saying that the missing number is 73 we do not know.'[2]

The company's misinformation was supported by Peter Ford. He said:

We know the number of people who travelled on the ferry because we double-count everybody and there were 543 on that ship. It is possible there may be a few who were hiding behind a car seat or were in the back of a lorry and were missed, but no more than a few.

Ford later added to the muddle by admitting:

We know there could be a duplication of names. It was a confusing scene and in some cases corrections were made. It could be that because of confusion we may have listed more survivors than there were and that in the end the death toll could be nearly 200. We can only hope that that will not be the case although it is true that 165 have already been recovered and clearly there are still more bodies on board.[3]

Townsend's inability to say for certain how many people were on board and how many had died undoubtedly caused great anguish to many relatives. Their alarm would probably have been even greater if they had known of a confidential Kent police report which claimed Ford said:

We are in the business of reassuring people, we want to give as much good news as we can and as soon as we can. If we tell 100 people that their relatives are safe and in ten cases we are wrong, then that is unfortunate. We have upset ten people but they would have been unhappy anyway, but we have at least made 90 people happy at an early stage.[4]

Ford vigorously denied this accusation and was supported by Sterling, who wrote in *The Daily Telegraph* on 9 April 1987: 'I believe that our efforts to deal with the aftermath of this tragedy have been wholly responsible, humane and deeply concerned to do everything possible to assist in a situation where we can recognise that all our efforts can do little to bring comfort to the mourning relatives.' He went on to talk of 'our resentment to the imputation that we are seeking to evade responsibility or lacking moral courage'. Despite such pleading there is little doubt that P&O's obstinacy in sticking to figures discounted by the police's findings gave the impression of a company keen to play down the dreadful consequences of the disaster.

The unhappy business of compensating survivors and next-of-kin gave P&O the chance to project a somewhat better image in the months following the disaster. At the time of the *Herald*'s capsize, the Athens Convention, to which Britain is a signatory, had imposed an upper limit of £38,500 on claims for loss of life in a maritime accident unless caused by recklessness on the part of the shipping company. Despite the erosion of its value by inflation, this had not changed since the 1970s. In May 1987 Parliament took unilateral action in raising it to £80,000. P&O then publicly announced that it was prepared to go up to the new maximum figure and even beyond it in cases of severe hardship. The company also decided to disregard the standard court figure for bereavement, then £3,500 and restricted to victims under the age of 18.

Ex-gratia payments were made very quickly from an emergency fund set up by P&O: £1,000 to survivors and £2,000 to next-of-kin. Just before the adjourned inquests were resumed in September 1987 several 'basic' payments were agreed with the steering group of solicitors representing most of the bereaved families. These included £5,000 for a victim's 'pre-death suffering' and a further £5,000 paid to his or her personal representative (normally next-of-kin).

Further claims for injury, loss of earnings and so on began to be dealt with individually in the New Year. No figures were disclosed, but it is understood that the largest payment (in a case involving the loss of parents of several young children) was about £165,000. Claims for nervous shock (post-traumatic stress disorder) went to arbitration early in 1988. Some had yet to be settled four years later. The company refused to accept arbitration of these claims by close relatives who had not been on the vessel but had watched the tragedy unfold on their television screens. (That is an issue which remains to be resolved satisfactorily following the House of Lords' recent rejection of an appeal by relatives of victims of the Hillsborough football stadium disaster.)

Back in 1987, Sterling publicly referred to P&O's generous treatment of Zeebrugge victims – a claim justified by the fact that the company had done a good deal more than it had been legally required to do. His public relations staff did not try to make too much of this, probably because they realised that a public accustomed to massive payouts in libel actions would not be impressed to find a young person's life valued at £10,000.

What are P&O frightened of – the truth?

A series of public relations fiascos followed the drama of the inquests. In February 1988 P&O wrote to all of its masters and officers at the time when the police began carrying out their investigations following the coroner's court verdict of unlawful killing:

> It may be of interest to you to know that our solicitors have advised us that although, of course, there is a civic duty on any citizen to assist the police in the prevention or detection of crime, there is no legal duty upon any citizen to assist the police and it is not an offence to refuse to give an interview to the police.[5]

Sam McCluskie, general secretary of the National Union of Seamen, responded with a pointed accusation: 'What are P&O frightened of – the truth?'

Long after the disaster, P&O continued to make headlines for the worst of reasons. In March 1988, it was disclosed that the company had still not paid the Red Cross for its work and help during Zeebrugge. Within hours of the tragedy the charity had organised 368 volunteers to provide food, clothing and comfort to survivors; it also provided ambulances, first-aid posts, lodging house and information points. Its bill, for £27,000, was submitted in November 1987. When the non-payment came to light, P&O European Ferries managing director Graeme Dunlop promised the cheque would be in the post. 'I don't understand how this has happened,' he said in a staff letter, a comment which could be seen as the management's motto.

Sterling did at the very least a bad PR job

The company was understandably anxious to put the events of 6 March behind it. Sometimes it seemed too anxious. It speedily dropped the name Townsend Thoresen and, in July 1987, became P&O European Ferries. 'There are really four reasons for working on an organisation's name. There are the mergers and acquisitions – of which the Liberal Democrat fiasco is a textbook example of how not to do things; there are the new launches; the companies changing direction; and the emergency first-aid projects,' wrote Simon Patterson of corporate identity specialists Wolff

Olins in *The Times* in March 1989. He went on to label the Townsend name change an 'emergency first aid project', comparable to Windscale's name change to Sellafield, an earlier attempt to reverse a poor public image. P&O dropped the name 'Free Enterprise' from all its ships – the *Spirit of Free Enterprise* became the *Pride of Kent* and other Free Enterprise ships became the *Pride of Hythe*, the *Pride of Sandwich* and the *Pride of Walmer*.

Only two weeks after the end of the inquests P&O launched a 'major media marketing campaign'. It also took the opportunity, at the same time, to complain about new safety measures proposed by the government, claiming that the adoption of these would 'axe' half of Britain's existing fleet of 62 coastal ferries. Its advertising company was given a brief to produce 'a campaign that assures people it is safe to go back on the water, but without reminding them why they may have doubts in the first place'. The result was a £1 million television advertising campaign showing a car winding its way through picturesque French country lanes. 'If you had a car all this could be yours,' the advertisement proclaimed. The advertisements did not feature a ferry.

Even with a variety of new names, a marketing budget and a public relations adviser, P&O found it a struggle to right its public reputation. In February 1988 the company invited families to sail across the Channel to a memorial service and then board a ferry to take them to the scene of the disaster. A P&O spokesman disarmingly said: 'We feel this is the caring thing to do. We hope our gesture will be appreciated.'[6]

P&O's attempts to put a positive glow on every occurrence sometimes defied logic. After a series of fires on its vessels early in 1988, managing director Graeme Dunlop proclaimed that the public had been 'greatly reassured' by the speed with which the latest fire had been doused. Later the company withdrew into silence, refusing to take part in a Channel Four programme on the safety improvements introduced since Zeebrugge.

Communication: the last refuge in case of disaster

The increasingly high media profile of Sir Jeffrey Sterling failed to assuage doubts about P&O's willingness to accept practical responsibility. If anything, it helped to draw on to P&O itself the obloquy that had previously been concentrated on Townsend.

A profile of Sterling in *The Daily Telegraph* on 27 April 1988, a year after Zeebrugge, noted: 'The sole blot on his copybook has been his handling of the Zeebrugge disaster ... Sterling did at the very least a bad PR job, offering scant compensation to the bereaved and appearing over-ready to let the ship's officers carry the can.' The second part of this comment referred to an interview on the BBC's *World at One* on 9 October 1987, when Sterling said: 'I think it gets a bit far-fetched that somebody sitting on shore should be hauled up.'

The communications issues raised by Zeebrugge reflect on the ship-ping and transport industries in general and go to the root of many of the problems underlying the actual disaster. Within the ferry business, dan-gerous incidents such as near misses remain closely guarded secrets. Ship owners and masters are now encouraged to report dangerous occurrences to the Marine Accident Investigation Branch (MAIB) of the Department of Transport. In 1988/9 the department carried out 85 investigations into near misses. That, however, is the extent of the public information.

Any Tom, Dick or Harry
can claim to be a ship designer

The MAIB, set up under the Merchant Shipping Act in 1989 after Zeebrugge, reports on 'more important marine accidents'. Its inquiries are conducted privately and written submissions are received in confi-dence. Ship owners and masters who make reports can ask for records of their identity and the names of the ships involved to be destroyed. As part of the Department of Transport, the MAIB's claim to be an independent watchdog seems weak. Between July 1989 and January 1990, it investi-gated 13 accidents which occurred on passenger boats. The findings are all confidential; summary reports are available only to those with a 'legitimate interest', a euphemism for those in the shipping industry. Incidents such as two accidents within three days on the ro-ro ferry *Pride of Kent* which resulted in 'accident to person' remained unreported to the wider public.

Professor Ken Rawson of RINA draws a comparison between the aviation and maritime approaches to communications.

The Civil Aviation Authority licenses operators and maintainers and enjoys the confidence of similar authorities worldwide. It publishes comprehensive and reliable statistics which may demonstrate trends that portend disaster and nip them in the bud. Designers worldwide, maintainers, operating companies and the pilots themselves all report, so that a total information system is available upon which safety matters may be judged.

In maritime safety, the Department of Transport states not the problem but the answer. Complex regulations lay down figures that have to be achieved which are often only incidentally and simplistically concerned with actual behaviour. Any Tom, Dick or Harry can claim to be a ship designer and expect to sell designs which satisfy these numerical criteria ... Secrecy surrounds much of the activity and few statistics are made available in the interests of safety. Indeed, no information system by which to judge trends exists. While certificates of safety are issued to the ship, operators are not licensed and may be regulated by their registration authority on the other side of the world.[7]

Secrecy also pervades the work of the Marine Directorate – the maritime regulatory section of the Department of Transport. The improvement and enforcement notices it issues are secret. The notices enforce a range of safety requirements including lifeboats, lifejackets, fire equipment, boat construction and pollution control equipment, as well as accommodation for crew and passengers. The public is unable, as a result, to discover which ships are persistently contravening safety regulations or how serious the breaches are. A total of 60 ships was detained in 1988/9, but their identity and type remain unknown.

Britain allows a period of three months before a second-hand ship brought on to Lloyd's Register has to be surveyed. This is a generosity open to abuse.

The IMO is also short on information. In 1991 its secretary-general revealed that it had received only 701 of 1,239 reports requested on serious casualties since 1978. 'The IMO cannot continue on the basis of business as usual in the face of this continuing loss of life, ships and property at sea,' he admitted.[8]

In the Channel specifically, there is reticence to take any action following incidents, even though they are occurring in one of the world's busiest sea lanes. Between 1982 and 1985, the Channel Navigations Information Service at Dover reported 474 contraventions of the collision regulations, including 63 by British ships. There was only one successful prosecution in those four years.

The lack of information – particularly to the public – stretches down to local and regional organisations. The Port of London Authority was asked by the Marchioness Action Group to give details of collisions which had occurred in the Thames prior to the one which sunk the *Marchioness* riverboat and killed 51 people in 1989. It was told that 44 collisions had occurred in the previous ten years. All requests for further details were refused because, though the authority compiles summaries of incidents, they are not available to the public.

Shipping statistics tend to be unhelpful too. Statistics on the gross tonnage of the most obscure ships are readily available, but figures are hard to find when it comes down to damage to property, injuries and deaths at sea. Lloyd's Register of Shipping, the most important source of shipping information, publishes extensive statistics on the losses of ships. Those on losses of life at sea, however, are confined to those from 'total' losses of ships – they do not include 'partial' losses which merely involve damage. Moreover, the deaths recorded are only those reported to Lloyd's. Deaths caused by other accidents are excluded. The IMO publishes no such statistics. The International Labour Organisation is similarly silent.

In the UK, the Department of Transport and the GCBS produce statistics on losses at sea, but as these only cover the UK they do not give a truly representative picture of safety. The consequence is that there is no measure of the success of the International Convention for the Safety of Life at Sea.

It is little wonder, given this carefully constructed veil, that a maritime consultant can comment:

> The general public, I would suggest, still don't see ships as dangerous. When you take off or land in an airliner, I would suggest there is at least a slight air of apprehension in the cabin. When a ferry sails there is no such feeling; so I think we will probably, even after the *Herald*, have to convey to the general public that ships can be bad for your health.

The overseeing bodies of other transport industries are more forthcoming with accident statistics. The reports of the Railway Inspectorate can be examined by the public. The Civil Aviation Authority has released information about air misses and dangerous occurrences since 1988. The ICAO *Statistical Yearbook* gives details of accidental deaths of crews and passengers and includes the types of operation concerned.

Only when the habit of secrecy disappears from the shipping industry as a whole will individual companies recognise the need for greater openness, and also the commercial advantages of such openness.

References

1. *The Sunday Times*, 15 April 1990.
2. *The Daily Telegraph*, 9 April 1987.
3. Ibid.
4. Kent police report, 19 May 1987.
5. Letter from P&O, February 1988.
6. *Daily Mirror*, 11 February 1988.
7. *The Human Element in Shipping Casualties*, Marine Directorate, 1991.
8. *Lloyd's List*, 14 May 1991.

CHAPTER NINE

Unlawful Killing

'Few people ... would accept a situation in which no one was held
to account for this disaster'
– New Law Journal.

'I intend to direct the jury that the concept of corporate manslaughter is
unknown at present'
– coroner Richard Sturt.

Britain's biggest-ever inquest, into the deaths of 188 of the *Herald*'s
victims, began on Monday 7 September 1987 at Dover Town Hall. More
than a thousand statements had been taken by the police before it began
under the Kent coroner, Richard Sturt.

'You face a very distressing and demanding task. You are going to
hear some of the most harrowing tales ever heard in a British court,' Sturt
warned the eight men and three women of the jury after reading out the
names of the 188 victims. 'A potential verdict you might have to consider
– and perhaps the most controversial – is unlawful killing.' For that
verdict to be returned, Sturt explained, the jury needed 'to be satisfied
beyond any reasonable doubt that the act or omission by an individual
caused, subsequently, one or more of the deaths and that the individual
was guilty of gross negligence'.

The boundaries of the inquest were confined

The parameters explained to the jury were quite different from those in
place up to 1977, when the Criminal Law Act substantially changed the
coroner's role. Before then, the coroner or the jury, after hearing the
evidence, had to return a verdict in which they were obliged to set out in
writing, as far as it had been proved, who the deceased was, how, when
and where they came by their death; and – if they came by their death by

murder, manslaughter or infanticide – the persons, if any, whom the jury found guilty of the offence. Where a coroner's inquest charged a person with murder or manslaughter, the coroner also had the power to issue a warrant for the arrest or detention of that person, if a warrant had not already been issued. All this was abolished by the 1977 Act. Today, the jury is not allowed to name any person it considers guilty and the verdict cannot be framed in such a way as to attribute any criminal liability to any named person.

While Sheen had, to a large extent, switched the burden of interest and blame from members of the crew to the company itself, Sturt made it clear that the boundaries of the inquest were confined by law, and by his interpretation of the law. He refused to call five directors of the company on the ground that they were too distant from the actual events for their evidence to be important. The evidence given by the only director called, Jeffrey Develin, was restricted to the system operated by the crew and to the procedure of trimming by the head (weighing down the bow of the ship with water ballast) at Zeebrugge.

Too remote from the disaster
to take any direct responsibility

Lawyers acting on behalf of some of the *Herald* families applied to the Divisional Court of the High Court in an attempt to overturn Sturt's decision not to allow other directors to be called. They wanted the jury to have a chance to decide whether the company itself was guilty of corporate manslaughter. Their appeal was rejected, but the court said it was 'tentatively' prepared to accept that, given the right circumstances, a limited company could be guilty of manslaughter – a possibility that the coroner had completely ruled out. However, the three judges suggested that, in this case, the directors were 'too remote from the disaster to take any direct responsibility', and that 'the case against a corporation can only be made by evidence properly addressed to showing guilt on the part of the corporation'.

The decision – or lack of any real decision – allowed Sturt to press on, keeping to his own interpretation of who was relevant to the case. 'It would be a radical and dramatic direction for me to give to the jury, that a company could be so directed [for corporate manslaughter],' he said. 'I therefore intend to direct the jury that the concept of corporate manslaughter is unknown at present to the law.'

Sturt later commented that 'the coroner has a difficult task in determining the scope of an inquest'. At the Zeebrugge inquest, he chose to concentrate on the conduct of individuals directly involved with the capsize rather than on broader questions of managerial or corporate responsibility. He also seems to have decided quite early in the proceedings that no criminal offence had been committed.

This approach is not an unusual one. At the hearing into the Clapham rail crash in 1990, the coroner, Dr Paul Knapman, similarly instructed the jury to rule out corporate manslaughter. 'The chain of events causing these deaths is of almost infinite length,' he said. 'I rule that if you are minded to return a verdict of unlawful killing and name British Rail as the perpetrators, as a matter of law I direct you that it is not open to you.'

Sturt was also doubtful about the possibility of verdicts of unlawful killing. Such verdicts are rare, but not unheard of. Normally, if it appears from the evidence given at an inquest that criminal offences may have been committed, the coroner is obliged to adjourn the hearing immediately and refer the papers to the Director of Public Prosecutions, who will then decide whether criminal charges should be brought. Unlawful killing verdicts usually occur when the assailant is dead or his or her identity is unknown. 'It is my intention to leave the verdict of unlawful killing to the jury,' said Sturt, before adding, 'I consider that a verdict of unlawful killing may not necessarily be found by the jury.' He laid down three essential elements with which the jury had to be satisfied to return that verdict. First, the 'act or omission of an individual ... was a substantial cause of death'; second, 'did that act or omission create an obvious and serious risk of causing physical injury?'; and finally, 'did he do so either without giving any thought to the possibility of that risk, or having recognised that the risk existed, having decided to take that risk?'

Few people in this country would accept
a situation in which no one was held
to account for this disaster

In summing up, the coroner reinforced the point that, in his opinion, Townsend directors were 'too remote from what happened to be accused of gross negligence'. The jury was sent out to consider its verdicts after 12 hours of summing up in the fifth week of the hearing. It took them several hours to reach unanimous conclusions.

The first verdict was read out soon after 4pm on Thursday 8 October. The verdict for all but one of the victims (a woman who died some time after the actual event) was unlawful killing. Given the coroner's instructions and advice, this came as a surprise. It was, however, widely approved. 'Few people in this country would accept a situation in which no one was held to account for this disaster,' commented the *New Law Journal* on 16 October 1987, before going on to express some dissatisfaction at the way the case had been handled. It doubted the true power of the coroner and called for coroners 'to have more teeth or for the matter to be referred at an earlier stage to someone who has'.

More caustically, *Private Eye* observed on 24 October 1987: 'The whole episode proved to the legal establishment how very unsafe juries can be and how the majesty of the law can be imperilled by a handful of ordinary people who are too easily swayed to sympathy at the thought of 200 innocent travellers unnecessarily killed.'

Following the verdicts, it was not surprising that there were calls for directors and the company to face charges. The *Daily Mail* said on 20 October 1987:

It's been laid down in law that the people responsible in such matters are those directing the minds and policy of the company. Develin and Ayers were responsible for the safety of the company fleet. If a system of positive reporting had been introduced, this disaster would not have happened.

Sir David Napley (who represented one of the families at the inquest) said there was 'not the slightest doubt' that a corporate manslaughter charge could be brought against the company. Sam McCluskie of the NUS commented:

If there is to be any prosecution, it should be against the company for allowing a system of work which cost the lives of 188 people when an individual overslept. The crew members in question were following work practices and procedures known to, and even condoned by, Townsend's senior management ashore.

The union considered taking out a private prosecution against the company, although nothing came of this.

P&O chairman Sir Jeffrey Sterling appeared to take a surprisingly relaxed view of the verdict. 'I think when one takes account of what transpired I can't think that they could arrive at any other than the verdict,' he said.[1] Given this acceptance of the verdict as all but inevitable, it was something of a turnround when, four days later in a message to P&O staff worldwide, Sterling said that 'no good purpose' would be served by prosecutions.[2] Sterling's statement on the 'inevitability' of unlawful killing verdicts (which would lead almost automatically to a criminal investigation) raises a further question regarding his company's readiness to cooperate with the authorities in fully investigating the disaster.

While the inquests were still in progress, the *Herald of Free Enterprise*, renamed *Flushing Range* and with its bow doors prudently welded together, was quietly towed through the Straits of Dover on its way to a scrapyard in Taiwan. It broke loose at least twice but was recovered. Members of the Kent police had to fly to South Africa to inspect the renamed ship, which many would have regarded as an important piece of evidence in a criminal investigation.

References

1. BBC *World at One*, 9 October 1987.
2. *The Daily Telegraph*, 13 October 1987.

CHAPTER TEN

THE MEANING OF 'OBVIOUS'

'Obvious: lying or standing in the way; open to (action or influence);
liable; plain and open to the eye or mind, perfectly evident; palpable.'
– Shorter Oxford English Dictionary.

'In layman's terms this was an open and shut case, but not so in
terms of legal technicalities.'
– Professor Michael Zander.

In November 1987, following the coroner's court verdicts, the then
Director of Public Prosecutions, Allan Green QC, ordered Frank Jordan,
Chief Constable of Kent, to carry out a criminal investigation into the
tragedy. Sixteen months later, after conducting hundreds of interviews
under the code-name Operation Libra, the Kent police sent its findings to
Green. He was left with the options of prosecuting the seamen; prosecuting the directors and senior managers (and through them, the company);
and ignoring widespread demands by doing nothing.

Business as usual

On 22 June 1989 a summons alleging corporate manslaughter was issued
against P&O European Ferries (Dover). For only the second time in a
British court, a company was to be charged with manslaughter. (The first
time was in 1964, when the Northern Star Mining Construction Company
was charged.) Also charged were seven individuals: two former Townsend
directors, Wallace Ayers and Jeffrey Develin; deputy chief marine superintendent John Alcindor; senior master John Kirby; Captain David Lewry;
first officer Leslie Sabel; and assistant bosun Mark Stanley. 'It has not
been an easy or a comfortable decision but we feel it is the right one,'
commented a spokesman from the Crown Prosecution Service (CPS) on
the decision to go ahead with the prosecutions. 'There is no doubt this is
an untested part of the law.'

96

The decision brought a strongly defensive response from Sterling. 'I do not believe that these charges are justified and our Dover company will fight them to the very limit with our full support,' he told P&O employees. 'I do not believe that any humanitarian purposes would be served by the prosecution of individuals. I repeat that to you today and wish to let you know that the company will stand behind all those involved.' P&O European Ferries managing director Graeme Dunlop told staff that it was a question of 'business as usual'.[1]

While Sterling's concern for individuals was no doubt commendable, it has to be borne in mind that a guilty verdict on Ayers, Develin, Alcindor and Kirby (and possibly Lewry, too) would have been a guilty verdict on the company, since any one of the senior defendants would be deemed to represent it. It also appeared that his assessment of 'humanitarian purpose' excluded the bereaved families, whose distress had been exacerbated by a sense of injustice because it seemed that no one was to be held to account for the 'unlawful killings'.

Even after P&O and the seven individuals were committed to trial by the chief metropolitan magistrate Sir David Hopkin, controversy continued as to whether it was just to charge P&O. Not surprisingly, given Sterling's avowal to fight the case to 'the very limit', P&O itself appealed against the decision. During a four-day hearing in July, its counsel argued that manslaughter could not be committed by a company because a company was not a 'natural person'. The appeal was rejected by Mr Justice Turner.

The High Court case opened on Monday, 10 September 1990. It was the first time that the directors of a company had stood trial in an English court for allegedly killing people by their reckless conduct though they were absent from the scene of the deaths. Instead of taking in all the victims, the charges named a single person: Alison Gaillard, 27 years old, who had been on a day trip to Belgium with her husband, who also died. A jury was sworn in from a specially enlarged panel of 145. They were asked a series of questions, some referring to their personal experience of ferry travel, and were warned that the case could last up to five months. When the trial got underway in Court No. 8 of the Old Bailey, the company and the seven individual defendants pleaded not guilty.

On the opening day Mr Justice Turner distanced the legal case from the actual event three and a half years before. He told the jury:

I am sure that some or all of you have some recollection of what you read in your newspapers or saw on your television screens at the

97

time and in the days following this great tragedy. You will, I hope and believe, find it possible to take entirely apart in your minds what you hear in this court by way of evidence as being the only evidence upon which your verdicts can be based. I tell you that is the only legal basis upon which you can proceed to reach your verdicts.

The judge also explained that the findings of a formal government inquiry and an inquest were not relevant to the present hearing. But when he mentioned the Sheen inquiry in his opening remarks to the jury he provoked outrage among the defence lawyers and some lengthy legal wrangling. After warning the jury not to be influenced by anything they had read or heard about the inquiry, Turner had commented that it 'pointed the finger at a number of individuals, some or all of whom may be before you in the court'. Defence lawyers quickly pointed out that their clients were not specifically blamed in the report. This altercation appeared to influence the general atmosphere in the court from then on.

The prosecution case eventually opened on the third day. David Jeffreys QC said:

The Crown's case is that the capsizing was avoidable and that each of the defendants that you are trying, the seven humans and the company, is responsible for the deaths that occurred because their behaviour or conduct was reckless and grossly negligent. The guilt of the company can only be established via the guilt of a directing mind. Hence, if you find one of those mentioned have committed the offence of manslaughter in the capacity of a person managing or directing the company, then the company likewise should be found guilty of the offence of manslaughter.

The challenge for the prosecution was to prove that at least one of the individual defendants was not only grossly negligent but reckless. For the company to be guilty, that individual had to represent its 'mind and will'. The judge made it clear that the criminal liability of the company could not be established by aggregating the acts of seven individuals which in themselves were not grossly negligent. Looking beyond its legal validity, that ruling had the effect of eliminating from the hearing the 'infection of sloppy management' so firmly diagnosed by the Sheen inquiry. It also seemed to distance the law from any perception of how businesses are run in the twentieth century. Crucially, the prosecution had to show that the recklessness of one or more individual defendants was in either not recognising or disregarding an obvious and serious risk that a ferry would sail with its bow doors open. But 'obvious and serious' to whom?

It was not obvious ... until it happened

After three weeks of evidence, the prosecutions' case was interrupted. It had called a succession of P&O masters. Not surprisingly, they all said they had not recognised the risk. After all, they were operating the same procedures as those on the *Herald* and were employed by the same company, the one in the dock. In effect, they became more effective as defence witnesses, backing up the defence's claim that any risks inherent in the system were far from obvious, even to experienced professionals. By calling the captains as witnesses, the prosecution drew attention away from managers ashore who actually installed the systems and should have been expected to have more of an overview of operational activities. Interestingly, the Sheen report made it quite clear that shore-based managers must have recognised the risk of one of their ferries sailing with its doors open. 'By the autumn of 1986 the shore staff of the company were well aware of the possibility,' it said.

At the Old Bailey, the judge had a different perspective. 'We have heard a weight of evidence to the effect that experienced seaborne personnel never thought for a moment that, with the system in force, there was any risk of that event happening,' said Mr Justice Turner. 'It was not obvious to any of those people until it happened; that is my intellectual difficulty.' The word 'obvious', with its various definitions, became the crux of the case. Turner continued:

> It is the essence of the case for the prosecution that before we get to the relevant state of mind of any one defendant there must have been an obvious and serious risk of the vessel putting to sea with her bow doors open in the light of the various alleged deficiencies.

His doubts sprung from four elements of the case which, in his view, made allegations of recklessness hard to prove. One of these was that the system had 'worked without mishap over seven years' (to quote the P&O counsel) in which there had been 'upwards of over 60,000 sailings ... about 5,000 on the Zeebrugge run'.

The law is rarely as simple as dictionary definitions

The inadequacies of Townsend's management and communication systems also worked in the company's favour. There was no evidence that four of the five incidents of ships leaving port with their doors open were known to the defendants. Finally, regulations imposed by the Department of Transport and Lloyd's did not require bridge lights. As the Sheen inquiry had concluded, the *Herald* was not breaking maritime law. As far as the regulatory bodies were concerned it was a safe ship. And if they regarded it as safe, how could the company and its employees think any differently?

The prosecution argued that it only had to prove that the risk was 'foreseeable by a reasonable person' for a jury to be able to decide that the risk was an 'obvious' one. Turner, on the other hand, made it clear that he was more persuaded by the company's counsel who defined an obvious risk as one which was 'perfectly evident' or 'stared one in the face'. There are a number of other definitions which, if accepted by the judge, would have altered the case considerably. The *Oxford Advanced Learner's Dictionary of Current English*, for example, defines 'obvious' as something 'easily seen or understood, clear; plain'.

Turner's narrow definition effectively debarred the court from considering two issues which many observers saw as particularly relevant to a case of such wide-ranging importance:

1. Did the known propensity of ro-ro ferries to capsize rapidly – with dreadful consequences – when water enters the car deck call for special care in designing the door-closing system and ensuring it was rigidly enforced?
2. Should the risk of a technically primitive system breaking down have been obvious to persons responsible for running a passenger transportation system of this magnitude?

After the end of the trial, a spokesman from the criminal operations branch of the Lord Chancellor's office commented: 'The law is rarely as simple as dictionary definitions, which themselves may differ between dictionaries.' Despite that protestation, semantics undoubtedly held the key to the prosecution's success or failure. Large amounts of evidence collected by the police failed to make their way into the prosecution case. The case remained, despite months in between, practically identical to the one put forward at the 21-day committal hearing in the magistrates' court, when the basis of the defence was well rehearsed.

The prosecution made no reference to the safety record of ro-ros and, aside from the masters, called no expert witnesses. The procedures of other companies were ignored – the judge would not allow the prosecution to call evidence from Sealink captains. 'The case has proceeded as I envisaged it would within its own tiny walls,' observed Turner. It was a case dominated by legal might. With more than 20 counsel in attendance, the court seemed to be concerned with containing – rather than fully exploring – issues of immense importance. The jury were continually excluded because of legal wrangles.

A week before the end of the case, Mr Justice Turner ruled that the words 'obvious and serious' meant 'the defendant's perception of risk was seriously deficient when compared to that of a reasonably prudent person engaged in the same kind of activity as that of the defendant'. In a legal ruling, with the jury absent, he concluded: 'There is no evidence that reasonably prudent marine superintendents, chief superintendents, or naval architects, would or should have recognised that the system gave rise to an obvious and serious risk of open-door sailing.'

Legal niceties have been upheld.
But what about justice?

The prosecution continued with its case, struggling against the fact that its witnesses had actually worked to the defence's advantage and the fact that the judge's interpretation of the key word differed substantially from its own. Aware that the judge was on the verge of dismissing the case, it accelerated desperately, calling 27 witnesses in just two days. In the end, only 66 of 138 prosecution witnesses actually gave evidence in court.

The case collapsed after 27 days, when the judge directed the jury to acquit P&O European Ferries and the other defendants except Sabel and Stanley. 'I have come to the very clear conclusion there is at this stage no evidence that would justify it being left to the jury to find that there was obvious and serious risk,' he said. The cases against Stanley and Sabel were dropped by the prosecution; proceeding solely against them was not in the public interest, it said. The judge then directed the jury to find them not guilty too.

Reaction to the end of the case produced a surprising consensus.

Maurice de Rohan of the Herald Families Association said: 'The real issues were not focused on in court. We had a lot of legal language and legal technicalities. The issue in our minds was to ensure that corporate responsibility went to the top level of the company.' The *Daily Express* said: 'Legal niceties have ... been upheld. But what about justice?' The *Daily Mail* observed: 'It seems that the more corporatist our society becomes the harder it is to make anyone carry the can.'

Politicians were similarly scathing. 'It seems the courts have confirmed that companies are not responsible for their actions in regard to the safety of their operations,' said shadow Secretary of State for Transport John Prescott.[2] Robert Adley, vice-chairman of the Conservative backbench transport committee, observed:

> Today's verdict ... highlights yet again the double standards which appear to apply in public transport matters, and emphasises the need for a review of the law as it relates to individual and collective liability.

There were some dissenting voices. 'I feel satisfied that this particular verdict has been reached. I have always felt that the prosecution was based on the report of the Sheen inquiry which contained many errors which were arrived at in the haste and emotion of the time,' said Jeffrey Develin (not going on to identify those 'errors'). Roger Mann, P&O's legal director, observed: 'While the company accepted from the outset responsibility for the passengers and their dependants, today's court decision confirms our view that there never was a case of corporate manslaughter.' Dover MP David Shaw later suggested that it was 'outrageously vindictive to pursue this case when the trial proved that the company did not commit manslaughter ... The error which caused the disaster was not deliberate and, in these circumstances, the judge had no option but to take this decision.'[3]

For many people, however, the law seemed irreconcilably distanced from public opinion. It was a gulf admitted by legal expert Professor Michael Zander of the London School of Economics: 'In layman's terms this was an open and shut case, but not so in terms of legal technicalities. The judge seems to have taken a very narrow legal view.'[4] Greville Janner QC, MP provided a straightforward response and solution: 'If the law is such that you cannot prove a case which appears to an ordinary human being to be so absolutely apparent, then the law should be changed.'

There was also concern over the trial's collapse because it seemed the desire of the judge to restrain it within its own 'tiny walls' infringed a number of basic liberties. Reporting was restricted and the media were not allowed to talk to bereaved families. There was even an attempt to obtain from the BBC and ITV companies an undertaking that they would not screen pictures of the disaster during the trial. The addresses of witnesses were withheld (a procedure usually only applied to 'super-grasses'), despite a 1987 Home Office assurance that such information would not be held back.

No question of a débâcle

The presentation of the prosecution case was also the subject of debate. Allan Green, then the Director of Public Prosecutions, had said: 'If you're prosecuting you make the running, you make the opening speeches.' In the *Herald* case, it seemed that the prosecution patently failed to 'make the running'.

On the power of a judge to abandon a case, the Lord Chancellor's office stated: 'A trial judge has the power and indeed the duty at an appropriate stage to direct a jury to return verdicts of not guilty against the defendants concerned if he considers that no reasonable jury, properly directed, could convict a defendant on the evidence before it.'

Responding to criticism, the Crown Prosecution Service said: 'There was no question of there being any débâcle. The prosecution, after much deliberation, put its case but, unfortunately, the judge had other views.'[5] There were also 'other views' on the performance of the prosecution counsel. The kindest adjective which could be ascribed to Mr Jeffreys's performance was 'uninspired'. His submissions and cross-examination appeared to lack a clear sense of direction. At one point the judge said he hadn't any clear idea of where the line of questioning was leading. 'My lord,' responded Jeffreys disarmingly, 'neither have I.'

The Attorney-General, Sir Patrick Mayhew, decided there was no point of law to warrant an appeal and the defence costs (all of which had been underwritten by P&O) were paid from public funds.

References

1. BBC Radio 4, *Shock Waves*, part 2, 18 April 1991.
2. *The Daily Telegraph*, 20 October 1990.
3. *Adscene*, 16 November 1990.
4. *Today*, 20 October 1990.
5. *The Times*, 20 October 1990.

CHAPTER ELEVEN

WHERE DOES THE BUCK START?

'Some of the people in the company are mere
servants and agents who are nothing more than hands
to do the work and cannot be said to represent
the mind or will. Others are directors and
managers who represent the directing mind
and will of the company.'
– Lord Denning.

'It says something about the moral climate in which we
live that a ship can sink, 188 people die, a judge
report a catalogue of negligence, a coroner's jury find
unlawful killing – and yet the owners can be so bold
as to contend that they, of course, are not to blame.'
– Hugo Young, *Guardian*.

More than three years before the collapse of the manslaughter trial, the
findings of the Sheen inquiry had begun to bring the management issues
into focus. The key question was forcibly expressed by MP Terry Dicks
in a dramatic House of Commons debate on 24 July 1987. 'How can
negligence at officer level be an offence, while negligence at company
level is not?' he asked the then Secretary of State for Transport, Paul
Channon. It is a question now engaging the attention of more and more
politicians, lawyers and business people.

A disaster like this was inconceivable

What do managers actually do? For what exactly are they responsible?
Where do their responsibilities begin and end – both legally and morally?
The answers are still clouded by the conventional divides between man-

agers and those who are managed. In some areas, managers are undoubt-edly keen to assume responsibility. Financial success, for example, is attributed to their strategy and wisdom. A good year in profit terms is triumphantly hailed by chairmen and managers as a measure of good performance. Poor results have also to be acknowledged but, of course, are likely to be put down to external difficulties such as the economy or a 'challenging' business environment. Responsibility becomes diluted fairly quickly.

When a disaster happens that, too, says something about a company's performance. In these circumstances managers are usually reticent in coming forward. At the higher levels, managerial heads rarely roll. There are exceptions – Sir Keith Bright and Dr Tony Ridley eventually resigned from control of London Underground after its management was criticised in the King's Cross inquiry. In general, responsibility is not so readily accepted.

Jeffrey Sterling resolutely refused to accept direct management responsibility for the Zeebrugge disaster. 'Those on board who were responsible to shut those doors did not carry out those instructions,' he said seven months after the disaster – after Sheen's critical findings and Townsend's acceptance of responsibility at the inquiry. Sterling seemed to have difficulty in accepting that managers remote from a company's activities could be held responsible for the mistakes of subordinates.

A refusal to countenance management failure is not unusual in such circumstances. 'It was a shock. A disaster like this was inconceivable. We pride ourselves on being safe. If established procedures had been fol-lowed this would not have happened.' So said Bill Stevens, president of Exxon, after its ship the *Exxon Valdez* spilled 11 million gallons of oil off the Alaska coast in 1989. The trouble was that by not following safety procedures, the company's employees made such a disaster conceivable and then, appallingly, reality. Senior management's perception of the company clearly differed from what actually happened in practice and the systems they managed failed to acknowledge human fallibility.

The board of directors must accept a heavy responsibility for their lamentable lack of direction

After the Zeebrugge disaster, other senior figures in the cross-Channel ferry business seemed to support Sterling. Sealink chairman James Sherwood suggested that 'failing to verify that the ship's bow doors were closed is as serious as the pilot and co-pilot of an aircraft failing to verify that they had fuel on board before taking off'.[1] The mistake was so basic that where the blame lay, he implied, was clear. A more direct analogy might have been with a plane taking off with its doors open – even the smallest aircraft have door warning lights as well as a very rigorous system of checks and double-checks.

Sterling's argument – like that of Exxon's Bill Stevens – was that once systems and procedures are in place, responsibility for following or ignoring them lies with the people on board. Management's responsibilities have been met by putting them in place. But what if the systems and procedures are inadequate or inappropriate, or have failed to take account of changes in technology or operating conditions?

In a roundabout way, P&O had faced up to the deficiency of Townsend's procedures. 'It is accepted by Townsend Car Ferries that their instructions could and should have contained an express instruction – but it was something that was so obvious that it scarcely needed saying,' said its counsel when the Sheen inquiry turned to the subject of the ship's standing orders. This half-hearted admission came about following an internal inquiry carried out immediately after Zeebrugge by P&O director Alec Black, two technical experts and a lawyer. Over ten days they interviewed survivors and examined the internal workings of Townsend. Their findings led to the decision to admit responsibility at the inquiry.[2]

Nevertheless, Sterling's interpretation of events, as shown by his statements to the media, ignored Sheen's conclusion that 'the board of directors must accept a heavy responsibility for their lamentable lack of direction. Individually and collectively they lacked a sense of responsibility. This left a vacuum at the centre.'

There was some evidence of muddled thinking. While arguing that responsibility did not lie with the company, Sterling readily admitted to the inadequacies of Townsend's management. He said in a convoluted radio interview:

Although there have been discussions and talk and accusations about sloppiness in the management of Townsend, I mean certain management aspects, I undoubtedly agree, and you can see from the fact that there's nobody at top level, of the original top, of Townsend, in place there today. But to suggest that they had a direct effect in that ferry capsizing in my view would be totally wrong ... Those on board who were responsible to shut the doors did not carry out those instructions, period. I think it gets a bit far-fetched that somebody sitting on shore should be hauled up in a similar context for that actually specifically not happening.[3]

Managers may be deficient, but Sterling appears to be arguing that this has no bearing on the behaviour or attitudes of those they manage. This is hardly an argument that would be supported, or even accepted, by the majority of professional managers.

All of this raises a basic question – one yet to be addressed by the law. In what circumstances does managerial sloppiness, even if it is rooted in incompetence, become a criminal offence? Sloppy management in a company making paper hats or garden gnomes is likely to affect only shareholders. Is a higher level of proficiency to be expected from those who take on the responsibility of running an operation to which millions of people entrust their lives every year?

Sterling argued that management had no responsibility for the disaster, but it was still felt necessary to make wholesale changes in Townsend's management team. 'The Zeebrugge tragedy will have quickened the pace of change at Townsend Thoresen. Change was going to happen anyway, but it will now happen vastly faster,' Sterling promised.

By August 1987 a Townsend spokesman was able to claim: 'None of the senior directors employed prior to the P&O acquisition remain with the company.' Wallace Ayers, by whom Sheen was 'singularly unimpressed', resigned. Jeffrey Develin, found by Sheen to have demonstrated an 'abject abdication of responsibility', also resigned. Others retired. The changes brought in a new managing director as well as a new deputy managing director, finance director and a director in charge of safety.

In a Radio 4 programme in 1991,[4] Develin reflected:

The size of the disaster meant that public emotions were running high. Somebody had to be seen to have made a mistake. There were a few of us who people decided were the guys ... I think everyone found it convenient to have a few Townsend executives and a few seagoing staff to be the scapegoats because you have a situation where it literally suits every other party and it puts the limelight on Townsend and not P&O. It was very convenient to all other parties.

Develin was also critical of Townsend's acceptance of responsibility at the Sheen inquiry. He, after all, was a director and might have hoped to have been party to any such decision reached by the company. 'I don't know to this day of any Townsend executive who was involved in making these concessions on behalf of Townsend Car Ferries,' he said. The instructions and decisions, he suggested, were coming from on high at P&O.

Sterling's comments in Autumn 1987 brought a fierce attack from Bill Mackey, a former receiver and liquidator who dealt with some of Britain's most notable corporate collapses, including Airfix, Laker and Stone-Platt. He wrote:

> I was surprised to hear Sir Jeffrey Sterling, chairman of P&O, say on the radio that people sitting in Dover could not be responsible for what happens on board ship. The answer of course is for the executives to get off their seats and go on the ship to find out what is happening.
>
> It should not be left to passengers or a coroner to let them know that the business is in serious trouble. Failures of a company's performance in all areas are the responsibility of management. If Sir Jeffrey believes his responsibility stops at the foot of the gangway the sooner he gives way to a manager who recognises the true depth of his responsibilities the better it will be for customers, employees and shareholders.[5]

Sterling's comments also drew a withering response from *Guardian* columnist Hugo Young. He came to broader conclusions, seeing Sterling's opinions and reaction as all too typical of attitudes to responsibility in public life as a whole:

> It says something about the moral climate in which we live that a ship can sink, 188 people die, a judge report a catalogue of negligence, a coroner's jury find unlawful killing – and yet the owners can be so bold as to contend that they, of course, are not to blame.[6]

The responsibility of command ... it will never change

Part of Sterling's conviction that there is no link between the activities of senior managers and crew on board ships comes from the traditional view of seafaring. Under this, the captain is sole arbiter of what happens on board his ship. It is a tradition P&O has sought to emphasise since

Zeebrugge. 'The responsibility of command has been something which has been a fact for hundreds of years and will never change,' Sterling proclaimed. 'I would like to think there is no officer in the P&O Group, or rating, who other than fully recognises the responsibility they specifically have for their passengers at sea.'[7]

The trouble comes when there is conflict between responsibility for passengers and the safety of a ship at sea *and* responsibility for overall corporate performance. In a landmark judgement in 1957, Lord Denning examined the idea of managerial responsibility. He said:

> A company may in many ways be likened to a human body. It has a brain and a nervous centre which controls what it does. It also has hands which hold the tools and act in accordance with directions from the centre.
>
> Some of the people in the company are mere servants and agents who are nothing more than hands to do the work and cannot be said to represent the mind or will. Others are directors and managers who represent the directing mind and will of the company.

In Townsend's case, responsibility for corporate success was, to some extent, loaded on the shoulders of the captains by putting them under pressure to achieve quick turnrounds. Using Denning's terminology, they were presumed to act as the brains and nervous system of the company. If a captain had, for safety reasons, ignored instructions to carry out such operations as quickly as possible, it is questionable whether he would have been wholly successful in relying on Sterling's faith in maritime tradition. Changes to standing orders after Zeebrugge seemed to pile more responsibility on the shoulders of the masters. Later in 1987, they threatened to work to rule in protest. 'Since the disaster, the company has issued more and more standing orders aimed solely at protecting the management,' argued the officers' union Numast. 'If the master is going to be held responsible for anything that goes wrong, he must protect himself.'[8]

The view that the captain is the person entrusted with total responsibility is not shared by others in the shipping industry. The president of the Nautical Institute, Commodore Gordon Greenfield (one of four assessors at the Sheen inquiry), explains the distribution of responsibility somewhat differently.

> A ship's master is ultimately responsible for the safety of passengers and crew, the ship and the cargo. However, to discharge this

responsibility the master must be given the authority to exercise his duties with respect to proper information and a properly trained crew who are in a fit condition to meet all the reasonable demands of the voyage ... In order for the master to discharge his proper responsibility, he must be supported by his company from ashore.

In practice, someone has to be responsible for the safety of a ship while at sea, but there is a substantial difference between that responsibility and the managerial responsibility of organising the safe and profitable running of a fleet of ships. Neither captains nor managers exist in a vacuum.

Sterling's interpretation of managerial responsibility also ignored the fact that the nature of managing the operations of a ship has changed considerably, as have so many other jobs. A ship is no longer isolated from the rest of the world when it is at sea. Instead, it relies on communications from land for information and much of its safety. Commanding an unwieldy ro-ro ferry with hundreds of passengers on board, a crew that changes from sailing to sailing, and a tight timetable to keep to is a far cry from commanding a vessel within the centuries-old traditions visualised by Sterling from his desk in Pall Mall.

The captain is responsible for people's lives,
not a balance sheet

The ferry's captain may be unable to recognise many of the crew and is reliant on company support services to ensure that the ship is in good running order. He may have responsibility for it during specific journeys, but the overall responsibility lies elsewhere. The job titles have remained the same, but the jobs themselves have changed dramatically with the passage of time and the influx of new technology. At the Sheen inquiry, David Steel QC, representing the Secretary of State for Transport, observed: 'It is not sufficient to delegate the tasks of rendering a vessel seaworthy entirely to the ship's staff.'

In general business terms, the captain could be compared to the manager in charge of a subsidiary. The central difference is that the captain is responsible for people's lives, not a balance sheet. There is little doubt that some measure of responsibility stretches down the line. Every job has an element of responsibility, no matter what it is. The paradox is that those with the least responsibility so often have the terms of their responsibility more clearly described for them than do those with ultimate responsibility. That was the case in Townsend Thoresen. The assistant bosun had responsibility for closing the bow doors; this was clearly laid out, even if not strictly applied. But the higher one progressed up the corporate ladder, the less well defined became areas of responsibility.

The irony of the situation is that the Townsend directors' failure to define their own duties, especially regarding passenger safety, became one of the company's principal shields in the criminal trial. Their argument was that if managers did not know, how could they or the company be held responsible? Taken to its conclusion, this argument means that some managers will not want to be told what subordinates are doing in case they are held personally accountable for it. It is a logic which is at the least irresponsible, and at worst outright dangerous.

---

*Only the shore management are in a position to monitor
operations, set high standards and impose
consistent and effective safety
procedures across their fleet*

Sterling's insistence that employees all traditionally have responsibility is questioned by Captain C. F. Spencer, managing director of Baltic Control:

> As a professional seafarer of many years, having worked on a variety of vessels including ro-ros on the cross-Channel routes, and having spoken to many of my colleagues at sea and ashore, I can never recall any officer at any time suggesting that any seaman up to and including the rank of bosun was ever 'responsible' for any act on any vessel. The officers of the vessel are the 'responsible' persons.[9]

It is interesting to speculate whether Sterling's insistence on the autonomy of the master, which identifies him as a 'directing mind' of the company, would have been put with so much force if Captain Lewry (whose Certificate of Competence had already been suspended by the court of inquiry) had been found guilty of recklessness at the criminal trial.

Sterling's interpretation of management and employees' responsibilities is not unique. Train driver Robert Morgan was jailed after his train killed five people when it went through a red light at Purley in 1989. The case provoked controversy. Morgan admitted the error from the very start (in the same way as the *Herald*'s assistant bosun never denied his crucial omission). 'The next time a powerful organisation can justly be held responsible for a terrible tragedy – be it land or air or sea – we doubt, we very much doubt, whether the man at the corporate controls will go to prison,' commented the *Daily Mail* on Morgan's sentence. Sentencing Morgan, the judge said: 'The railway passenger who gets onto a train puts himself in a very special sense into the hands of the driver.' The responsibility, however, stretches further than that. The railway company, too, is involved as it is responsible for the maintenance of the train, the systems surrounding its running, and the training and proficiency of its staff.

The parameters of responsibility are undoubtedly difficult to gauge. It is clear that companies which offer a service to the public have a duty to take sufficient care of the people who use that service. From there on, there is no consensus on what is 'sufficient', and on how, or even whether, the duty should be enforced. The role of individuals, whether managers or humble employees, in fulfilling this duty is, if anything, even vaguer.

That there is a relationship between management, captain and safety was cautiously accepted by Lord Brabazon, then Minister for Aviation and Shipping, in a House of Lords debate on merchant shipping in 1987:

> A ship that is not well managed by its master in terms of having clear lines of command and making sure that everyone knows what his duties are is not a safe ship. There is a limit to how much a master can achieve in this respect. There is an important role for shipowners and management companies.

Later, Brabazon went on to say: 'The Government fully accept that a sloppy and inefficient shipowner or ship's manager can make it very difficult for a master to carry out his duties safely.' 'Sloppy', of course, was the very word used by Sheen to describe Townsend's management. Determining where lines of responsibility fall was identified by Brabazon as an important step forward: 'The Government does believe that clarification of the duties and responsibilities of all those involved in the operation of ships is an important part of ensuring that we do not have further tragedies such as occurred to the *Herald*.'

The then Secretary of State for Transport, Paul Channon, also made the link clear:

> The Government believes that an effective legal framework for

maritime safety needs to place strict duties both on the master and the crew, and on the owner and management. Particularly in relation to intensive operations like the cross-Channel services, where just one ship can be operated by as many as five crews, only the shore management are in a position to monitor operations, set high standards and impose consistent and effective safety procedures across their fleet.

The role of management in safety is all the more important when the day-to-day activities of the company are as potentially hazardous as in the cross-Channel ferry business. The more complex the operation, the more managers are duty-bound to take responsibility for the complexity and safe running of it. For senior managers the challenge is to develop a comprehensive knowledge of the day-to-day activities of the company while retaining sufficient independence of mind to enable them to reach sound strategic decisions. One cannot exist without the other.

Professor A. R. Hall of the Safety Science Group at Delft University says:

> Creative and systematic thinking does not occur unless someone is given the time to sit down and indulge in it. That someone also needs sufficient knowledge of the system, as it is designed and, more importantly, as it will be used (and misused) in practice. They also need the detachment to be able to think as broadly as possible and not to be railroaded into rapid decisions about modifications to be made to prevent the last disaster.[10]

The captains of cross-Channel ferries, working long hours and having a heavy responsibility for operational matters, do not have the time to sit down and analyse the strategic operations of their company.

A high degree of autonomy

The difficulties in deciding where responsibility stops and starts were shown in the court case over County NatWest's involvement in the 1987 Blue Arrow rights issue. In court, Gavin Casey, formerly deputy chief executive of County, was cross-examined on his knowledge of the events. Casey, then earning a salary of £120,000 and having been awarded a bonus of £60,000, was asked what he was being paid for. 'Responsibilities? Taking decisions?' asked the counsel. 'I was paid ... a lot of money to do many things. Just because I was paid a lot of money, it did not mean I was heavily involved in all aspects of this,' said Casey.[11] He argued that he was not 'heavily involved' in the deal despite attending meetings on it and seeing a variety of notes on the subject. Casey was caught in an uncertain position between intimate, detailed knowledge on the one hand, and general awareness of events on the other.

This balance lies at the very heart of what managers actually do. While the law is based on precedents and is backward looking, management is concerned with anticipating events and planning accordingly – whether the event in question is a fall on the Stock Exchange or a failure of operational procedures. According to management guru Henry Mintzberg, managing involves three elements: managing continuity (staying on track), managing boundaries (staying in touch), and managing change (keeping up to date).

Townsend tried, unsuccessfully, to get the best of all worlds. It was claimed that its ships and managers were given 'a high degree of autonomy'. At the inquiry its counsel admitted it may have left too much to its senior masters. The trouble was that theirs was autonomy in name only. Jeffrey Develin admitted that he was not restrained by any financial guidelines; he discovered how much he could, and could not, spend through trial and error. He was restrained, if anything, by the vagueness of the system he operated under. In fact, Develin told the inquiry that becoming a director of the company in October 1986 made 'no practical differences to his responsibilities'.

Management responsibilities were vague and undermined

On board ship the management responsibilities of the masters were vague and sometimes undermined – in spite of Sterling's protestations about the history and permanence of lines of command. In effect, captains were allowed to manage when it suited the company. Part of the problem was that the professional expertise of the captains was not fully understood – or respected – by shore-based managers who were unqualified to deal with nautical matters.

Townsend's Marine Department originally had a nautical superintendent, an expert. When he left, he was never replaced. Typically, Develin came from an engineering rather than a maritime background. Ayers' decision not to bring a nautically qualified superintendent into his department simply accentuated the lack of expertise. Though they were ill equipped to deal with nautical matters, shore managers felt confident enough to interfere in operational issues.

Complete ignorance of the problems which existed

In July 1985, Captain Kirby, the *Herald*'s senior master, lodged a protest that senior management had 'advised' that penalties which had been correctly imposed should be rescinded because the crew threatened to strike. There had been a similar case on the *Pride of Free Enterprise*. Managerial responsibility was given to captains, yet when they came to exercise it their position was undermined. 'No master can maintain discipline in his crew unless he has the confidence and backing of the management,' said Sheen.

During the inquiry into the disaster of the *Piper Alpha* oil rig, the union representative argued that the gulf between management and what actually went on was similarly broad. He said:

> The whole management evidence from Occidental [the owners of the rig] paints a picture of complete ignorance of the problems which existed. The senior management provided no support to the platform staff. They provided no training. They provided no guidance. They laid no procedures. They did not participate in discussions with the operators. They did not seek the views of their employees.[12]

There is evidence of a similar divide within British Rail. Changes brought in new managers and marketers at the expense of rail specialists. A former area manager commented: 'Train crew strategy is conceived at business rather than operations headquarters. The cost in abortive route and traction learning has been enormous. Four train crew depots have been taught the Oldham loop line in the past three years, none of whom now drive round there.'[13]

Similar situations arise in management in many other areas. Financiers manage ferry companies; accountants manage engineering companies; marketers manage software businesses. Expertise in a particular business is no longer a prerequisite for success. As a relatively new discipline – in name at least – management covers a multitude of skills and occupations.

Defining what managers should do and what they are is complex. Usually unqualified – save for experience – they exist in a well-remunerated world of perpetual trial, error and self-justification.

---

*Management: distanced
from the reality of corporate performance*

Over the responsibilities of management there is legal confusion. A 1971 House of Lords case found that Tesco was not criminally liable when one of its shop managers defaulted on a payment. It decided that the manager was not sufficiently senior to count as the company. Judges have differed on what actually constitutes 'senior management'. Lord Diplock restricted it to directors; Lord Reid included senior officers who carry out the functions of management; Lord Dilhorne included persons in actual control of operations who in practice are not responsible to anyone else.

Unfortunately the fact that what management involves is commonly unclear can give the impression that managers are not subject to the same responsibilities and limitations as their employees. Management sometimes seems to manage in a vacuum, distanced from the reality of corporate performance.

The Fayed brothers' takeover of Harrods provides an example. Despite a DTI report claiming they consistently lied and misinformed government departments and shareholders, the brothers remain in charge of the retail business (although they were forced to give up control of Harrods' Bank). 'If a Harrods shop girl had obtained employment with the help of a bogus reference, she would expect to be sacked if the deceit was discovered,' observed *The Times* on 8 March 1990. Others had a different view, accepting lying as a business tactic. Reggie von Zugbach of Glasgow Business School argued:

> An entrepreneur who balks at misleading some jack-in-office, with no legal comeback, is clearly derelict in his duty. Such a person is not fit to have control of the property of others, for he is liable to place personal whim or scruple before the duty of care towards the assets in his charge. If the Fayeds lied to DTI officials, breaking no law, this must be judged as the normal and proper behaviour of competent and responsible entrepreneurs.[14]

One can only hope that this attitude is not being adopted by all business school graduates!

Of course, some senior executives take full responsibility when things go wrong. When a Japan Airlines Boeing 747 crashed in 1985, killing 520 people, the company's president resigned. Before doing so, he visited the families of every victim with traditional Japanese mourning gifts. He was helped by 17 senior managers, and 420 employees spent time giving assistance to the families of the victims. A government report later showed that the company itself was not directly responsible for the disaster. Faulty repairs carried out by Boeing and inadequate inspections by the Japanese transport ministry were, in fact, the causes.

Responsibility comes in diverse forms in other areas of life. In the political world, admitting to an error – whether political or personal – is virtually anathema. Resignations and dismissals tend to be ascribed to matters of principle rather than ineptitude or misjudgement. When asked what way to blame for the build-up of communal war in his country, President Jayawardene of Sri Lanka replied: 'My own lack of intelligence, lack of foresight and courage.' It would be difficult to find parallels in contemporary business of managers willing to accept such personal responsibility.

One thing is certain: the men and women at the top of a company provide role models for those they command. Demonstrations of personal responsibility influence the attitudes and behaviour of the entire organisation. So, unfortunately, do demonstrations of personal irresponsibility.

References

1. *The Times*, 23 May 1987.
2. *The Daily Telegraph*, 15 August 1987.
3. BBC *World at One*, 9 October 1987 (Tellex Monitors transcript for P&O Group Information).
4. BBC Radio 4, *Shock Waves*, part 2, 18 April 1991.
5. *The Daily Telegraph*, 14 October 1987.
6. *Guardian*, 13 October 1987.
7. BBC *World at One*, 9 October 1987.
8. *The Times*, 15 August 1987.
9. *Lloyd's List*, 15 January 1988.
10. Paper presented at Disaster Prevention and Limitation Conference, Bradford University, December 1989.

11. *Independent on Sunday*, 7 July 1991.
12. *Safety Management*, December 1989.
13. *Independent on Sunday*, 7 July 1991.
14. *The Times*, 17 March 1990.

CHAPTER TWELVE

LAW AND THE REAL WORLD

'Recklessness by jeopardising public safety should be a crime,
whether tragedy ensues or not. And the law should not make
it too difficult to prove.'
– editorial in *The Times*, 23 June 1989.

The poky public gallery of Court No. 8 at the Old Bailey was crowded
with relatives of Zeebrugge victims when the trial abruptly ended on 19
October 1990. There was no fuss. The relatives, however, were surprised
and dismayed – not just by the acquittal of the company but by the way
this had come about. To those who had climbed up to the gallery day after
day it seemed that the legal system had put insuperable obstacles in the
way of fully examining the corporate and management roles in the
disaster, and had suppressed issues which to them seemed entirely relevant.

The Kent police had spent 16 months collecting a huge volume of
evidence. The Director of Public Prosecutions had taken three months to
decide whether, by the tough criteria imposed on his service, it was right
to bring charges. The prosecution's case – and the defence's – had been
well rehearsed at the long committal hearing, when the legal obstacles
had begun to reveal themselves. The CPS had had a further nine months
to assess, and perhaps strengthen, its case. Now a judge was saying that in
his opinion there was nothing to put to a jury.

Defence counsel sought to recover their costs direct from the CPS (and
not simply from the public purse) on the ground that the case had been
either improperly or unnecessarily brought. This application Mr Justice
Turner eventually refused.

There was some talk of the Attorney-General referring the judgement
to the Court of Appeal but it soon fizzled out. A spokesman for the Law
Secretariat later explained (in a letter to the Herald Families Association):
'A study of the proceedings did not disclose a point of law of sufficient
general application to warrant that course.' Turner's ruling, he said, had
been based on 'evidential points directed very much to the circumstances
of the particular case'.

The case received only a small fraction of the coverage that recent City scandals had received

Experienced press reporters thought that the proceedings in Court No. 8 had been also wholly devoid of the 'atmosphere' of a criminal trial. The defendants sat not in the dock but beside their lawyers. The highest points of drama were when the judge displayed either exasperation or impatience with the prosecuting counsel. Someone visiting the Old Bailey during the trial would never have thought that the case had anything to do with the unlawful killing of a large number of persons. Media representatives, hedged in by contempt of court orders, had soon lost interest. The case received only a small fraction of the coverage that recent City scandals have received.

Such details are not directly relevant to the debates which are now taking place on the need for reform in this area of law, but they reflect the inclination of many people, often well meaning, to 'decriminalise' serious offences committed by companies and their senior officers. There is always liable to be a gap between an ordinary person's idea of justice and the justice administered by the legal system. This is particularly true where that ordinary person sees himself or herself as a victim of crime. But there is genuine cause for concern where the gap becomes too wide and is either unexplained or inexplicable.

In the case of laws affecting ferry design, the RINA's Ken Rawson says that 'a weak correlation between legislation and moral values has been normal in forming requirements for the design of ships for many years. Law to protect the sea traveller has been driven rather by disaster and public outrage.'[1] The Zeebrugge relatives' surprise at the outcome of the trial was not shared by the legal experts who had been watching. A typical comment came from Stuart Field of Cardiff Law School: 'It is perhaps ambitious to expect judicial innovation in the law relating to corporate manslaughter to succeed in the first instance.'[2] Of course, the dismay felt by the relatives was because resistance to judicial innovation seemed to be getting in the way of justice.

Safety campaigners – along with many others – had hoped that the prosecution of P&O European Ferries, regardless of the verdict, would do for corporate safety standards what the mere arrest of Guinness's Ernest Saunders had supposedly done for financial probity in the City. They saw it as an opportunity to send clear signals to company directors and managers that their conduct in areas other than finance was coming under closer scrutiny, and that they would face harsh penalties if it were found to have breached criminal law. The collapse – not just failure – of the prosecution could be construed as taking one step forward and two back. Turner's judgement not only enabled P&O to declare 'there never was a case of corporate manslaughter'; it seemed to be signalling to irresponsible directors and managers that in all probability there never would be one.

As a result of the Zeebrugge case ... corporate manslaughter is legally admissible as a charge in an English court. But it looks harder than ever to prove it

---

Michael Zander, professor of law at the London School of Economics, commented: 'As a result of the Zeebrugge case ... corporate manslaughter is legally admissible as a charge in an English court. But it looks harder than ever to prove it.'[3] Ivan Lawrence MP, chairman of the Conservative back-bench legal affairs committee, said: 'The difficulty with the charge of manslaughter is that you must prove that people who were, perhaps, two or three stages removed from the event, are culpable. The degree of negligence has got to be of a very high order.'[4]

The charge may be admissible, but it is still in a fledgling state in English law. Before the Zeebrugge prosecution, the only case that had been heard was at Glamorgan Assizes in 1964. This involved the Northern Star Mining Construction Company. The question of whether a company *could* be guilty of manslaughter was hardly raised, and Northern Star was acquitted. Outside the UK, the concept of corporate responsibility is often viewed differently. In the US, the Court of Appeal observed in 1987 that 'corporations compartmentalize knowledge, subdividing the elements of specific duties and operations into small components. The aggregate of those components constitute the corporation's knowledge of a particular operation.' That definition of how businesses are run may be unwieldy but it is a good deal closer to the real world than the perceptions of the protagonists in the Zeebrugge trial.

The American legal system also seems to accept that the collective knowledge of a corporation is not wholly derived from within its own walls. In 1985 three directors of Film Recovery Systems Inc. were found guilty of the murder of an employee, and the company itself was found guilty of involuntary manslaughter and reckless conduct. This was after failure to install the fume hoods which the individual defendants knew were regarded as essential for employee safety by other operators in their industry. It is interesting to compare that case with the Zeebrugge trial, during which it was ruled that Sealink captains could not be called as prosecution witnesses because the procedures and systems operated by other ferry companies had no relevance to what was done on the *Herald of Free Enterprise*.

> *The concept of aggregation was one of the main rocks on which the prosecution of P&O European Ferries foundered*

The key word in the pronouncement by the US Court of Appeal reported above is unquestionably 'aggregate'. The concept of aggregation was one of the main rocks on which the prosecution of P&O European Ferries foundered. That concept was firmly rejected by three divisional court judges in August 1987 when relatives of Zeebrugge victims sought leave to appeal against the ruling by the Kent coroner, Richard Sturt, that only individuals could commit manslaughter. Mr Justice Turner upheld that judgement at the criminal trial. He insisted that there was no question of making a company guilty of reckless conduct by combining the actions of individuals which in themselves were not reckless. The culpability of the corporate body had to be assessed on the conduct of a single person of a status that could be said to represent that body's 'mind'.

The aggregation concept, so obviously reflecting the conduct of business in the real world, has been recommended by the Council of Europe. In 1988 it declared that the acts of individuals should be accumulated when deciding whether or not a company has committed an offence.

> *The possibility of people being unlawfully killed as a result of a company's defective policies and practices tends not to be taken seriously*

In England a major impediment to reform is that at all stages of the legal system there appears to be an inbuilt presumption that companies as such do not commit serious crimes. A company can be taken to court for relatively minor breaches of legislation, such as inflicting grievous financial harm on its shareholders. It can be found sufficiently fraudulent, as in the case of the Bank of Credit and Commerce International, to be shut down. But the possibility of people being unlawfully killed as a result of a company's defective policies and practices tends not to be taken seriously. The logic behind this presumption of corporate innocence can probably be traced back to a bygone age when it was impracticable to punish a company for unlawful killing because the only penalty for that crime was hanging. Today, its effect is to inhibit the process of criminal investigation right from the start. It deters the police from conducting an examination of the kind that would be launched automatically if they were dealing with a traditional crime of violence.

When 31 people were killed and a further dozen seriously burnt by a fire at King's Cross Underground station on 18 November 1987 – almost immediately after the unlawful killing verdicts on the Zeebrugge victims – all the police looked for was evidence of either arson or terrorism. They did not see it as within their remit to investigate the possibility that the management had recklessly disregarded previous warnings, or had been grossly negligent in either providing the right equipment or training staff in fire-fighting methods. It was left to a coroner to decide there was no evidence of unlawful killing and to instruct his jury to return verdicts of accidental death. The same reluctance to investigate fully has been observed in most if not all the disasters which have happened this century.

When nearly two hundred people perished in the *Herald of Free Enterprise* the police role was initially restricted to the rescue operation and recovery of bodies. A criminal investigation was not considered to be necessary, despite all the prima-facie evidence of reckless conduct, until six months later. Then unlawful killing verdicts were returned by a jury which was probably expressing the public outrage generated by the revelations at the Sheen inquiry.

It could be argued that in this case the inaction of the police was reinforced when Mr Justice Sheen unequivocally pronounced that no criminal offence had been committed. But this does not logically explain why the police were not asked to move into the ferry company immediately after the capsize – perhaps with a dawn raid of the kind associated with cases of suspected fraud. Whether the delay had any effect on the outcome of the criminal trial three and a half years later it is impossible to say. But it is not unreasonable to think that during a period of several months, memories had dimmed. The fact that the criminal trial had been preceded first by a public inquiry and then by an inquest – the findings of which got wide publicity throughout the world – created further legal difficulties. That was demonstrated by Mr Justice Turner's inevitable instruction to the jury to put out of their minds whatever it was that had been found by those lower courts.

It is the recent spate of disasters ...
which has focused attention on weaknesses and
anomalies in the way the legal system deals
with possible cases of 'corporate violence'

Other disasters have been followed by even worse muddles in the timing of inquiries, leading to suspension of inquests and the suppression (at least temporarily) of technical reports. Neither of those devices, so clearly in conflict with the principle of freedom of information, would be needed if the authorities had a firm policy for finding out whether or not a disaster involved criminal misconduct.

In the case of the *Marchioness* disaster on 20 August 1989, a report was held back on the ground that its publication would prejudice the trial of the captain of the dredger that rammed the riverboat. He had been charged with the minor offence of failing to keep a look-out, and his trial was abandoned after two juries had failed to reach a verdict on the confused case presented to the court. The suppressed report was, however, published – presumably with no fear of prejudicing anything – after the Marchioness Action Group had announced its intention to initiate a private prosecution of the company owning the dredger and some of its directors. There was also a curious development when the Attorney-General threatened to take over that prosecution and quash it – a threat which, understandably, he withdrew when it was published and attacked in the press. (A private prosecution brought by the husband of one of the victims was dismissed by the Chief Metropolitan Magistrate at the committal proceedings in June 1992 although, surprisingly, his full costs were paid by the court.)

It is the recent spate of disasters – commanding great public interest – which has focused attention on weaknesses and anomalies in the way the legal system deals with possible cases of 'corporate violence' resulting in multiple deaths and injuries. But these same weaknesses and anomalies have long existed in the treatment of individual death or injury at work.

In May 1970 the Labour Secretary of State for Employment and Productivity, Barbara Castle MP, appointed a committee to 'review the provisions made for the safety and health of persons in the course of their employment ... and to consider whether changes are needed'. One of the eventual conclusions of that committee was that 'the traditional concepts of criminal law are not readily applicable to the majority of infringements which arise under this type of legislation'. Death, the committee seemed to be saying, was often the result of an infringement or carelessness or inadequate supervision rather than either negligence or recklessness by an employer with an obvious responsibility to foresee and prevent such things. It may be of significance that the chairman of this committee was Lord Robens. As chairman of the National Coal Board at the time of the Aberfan disaster, he had been criticised for his attempt to deny management responsibility, and also for giving unclear evidence on corporate knowledge of the geological fault beneath the coal tip which engulfed the village school, killing 116 of its pupils.

---

*Prosecutions for unlawful killing
are less common,
one suspects, than the crime itself*

It is unfortunate that over the years many trade unions – including those in the accident-ridden construction industry – have tended to subscribe to the same values as the employers by concentrating on compensation for death or injury rather than on measures for eliminating the unsafe practices which currently claim some six hundred lives a year. Sadly they are only awakening to their full responsibility for workplace safety now that their strength is at a low level.

Health and safety at work offences are handled by the HSE. This body normally prosecutes companies rather than individual directors (because it finds it easier to get convictions with the former), but most of its prosecutions are for breaches of safety regulations rather than 'crimes of violence'. It rarely refers cases to the crown court and even more rarely asks for a police investigation. There is a widespread impression that the HSE is 'soft' on corporate wrongdoers and prefers to persuade rather than punish. Its officers strongly reject this image and point to the rising number of convictions they have secured in recent years. But prosecutions for unlawful killing are less common, one suspects, than the crime itself.

One notable instance of the HSE collaborating with the police in an investigation of workplace death occurred in 1988 when an employee of a plastics company was dragged head-first into an inadequately guarded crumbling machine. This resulted in one of the company's directors being successfully prosecuted for manslaughter. He got a suspended two-year prison sentence. A second director, who was said to spend less time on the shopfloor, was fined only £15,000 on a lesser charge even though the judge made it clear that he should have known of the unsafe practices operated by his company.

The image of the HSE as a reluctant prosecutor, especially for serious criminal offences, has partly arisen from its own statements of policy. 'Inspectors do not approach their task with a view to seeking out legal violations and prosecuting errors. They seek to promote reasonable compliance with good standards,' it said in its annual report for 1990. Its director-general, John Rimington, has said that he 'wouldn't subscribe to the idea of treating health and safety offences as normal criminal offences'. In 1990 he told a Commons select committee on employment: 'A bloodthirsty attitude is not the right one to take.' Later he gave an assurance that this was not a reference to the impending prosecution of directors and managers of P&O European Ferries. HSE chairman Sir John Cullen was less negative at that Commons committee meeting. He accepted there were certain circumstances when a jail sentence would be more appropriate as a punishment and deterrent than a fine. An issue on which Rimington has expressed concern is the low levels of fines imposed on wealthy companies by magistrates and crown court judges. Welcoming the recent rise in the maximum fines permitted by law, he reflected that 'we were getting to the situation where the law was specifying higher penalties for the death of bluebells than people'.

---

*Offence and punishment often seem
to be almost ludicrously out of proportion
to each other*

There is a certain irony in the fact that the HSE was not involved in either of the two biggest cases of workplace deaths in recent history – the loss of 38 crew on the *Herald of Free Enterprise* and the loss of 191 oil rig workers in the *Piper Alpha* explosion. The former came under the Department of Transport, the latter under the Department of Energy – although that responsibility has since been transferred to the HSE on the recommendation of the court of inquiry into the disaster.

The HSE did act in the case of the 1988 Clapham rail crash after the Director of Public Prosecutions decided there was insufficient evidence to warrant a prosecution for manslaughter. As a result British Rail was fined £250,000 for exposing passengers to danger. The judge pitched the fine at that low level after the defence pointed out that the whole amount would have to come out of the pockets of rail travellers.

Offence and punishment often seem to be almost ludicrously out of proportion to each other. In July 1991, for instance, the P&O company Bovis Construction was fined just £1,000 after a workman died on one of its sites. He was the fourth to do so in 18 months. Even the £750,000 fine imposed by a Scottish court on British Petroleum for the failure of safety precautions at its Grangemouth refinery, which resulted in three deaths, is small beer when compared with the company's revenue and profits.

What the future holds is not yet clear, but changes are in the air. The prosecution of P&O European Ferries, although sometimes portrayed as a fiasco, will eventually prove to have been much more significant than that. By its very failure within the 'tiny walls' of Mr Justice Turner's court, it drew attention to weaknesses in the legal system which have been tolerated for far too long. This has happened, perhaps not coincidentally, at a time when the integrity of the legal system has been brought into question by a spate of wrongful convictions and allegations of illegal acts by police investigators. The result has been the appointment of the first Royal Commission on Criminal Justice for many years.

Surprisingly, the initial programme drawn up by the Royal Commission did not take account of the public unease created by the treatment of possible crimes of corporate violence in the Zeebrugge and other disasters. But its terms of reference are certainly wide enough to accommodate such matters. They are 'to examine the effectiveness of the criminal justice system in England and Wales in ensuring the conviction of those guilty of criminal offences and the acquittal of those who are innocent, having regard to the efficient use of resources'.

A submission to the Royal Commission by the charitable organisation Disaster Action includes evidence of the 'embedded bias within the criminal justice system against treating corporate crimes of violence as seriously as it treats individual crimes of violence'. One of its recommendations is that multiple deaths or injuries arising from corporate activity should be immediately investigated by the police for evidence of criminal behaviour. That alone would resolve some of the confusion that has occurred in the wake of recent disasters.

> *The system for investigating possible crimes of corporate violence should be modelled on that ... for investigating fraud*

The HSE has reservations about the value of police investigations in all but the most severe cases. It believes that this could result in workers, rather than directors, being hauled up in front of the courts. The police would be interested in 'who is holding the smoking gun', whereas the HSE looks at the organisational structure behind an accident, according to one of its spokesmen. There is some substance in that argument, but it would be better if the HSE were to see it as an obstacle to be overcome rather than a reason for not making changes.

Disaster Action's submission recognised this danger. It therefore suggested that the system for investigating possible crimes of corporate violence should be modelled on that already in place for investigating fraud. To be effective the police conducting the investigation would need specialised knowledge of organisation structure and management practice. Disaster Action proposed the establishment of 'corporate violence units' attached to regional police forces. These would immediately investigate possible crimes of negligence or recklessness resulting in individual deaths or injury. To deal with multiple deaths, as in recent disasters, there should be a 'serious corporate violence office' operating in much the same way as the present Serious Fraud Office.

It is not within the Royal Commission's terms of reference to consider the creation of new criminal offences. But the unsatisfactory treatment of disasters had made lawyers and others increasingly aware of the need for reform in that area.

The people calling for change include lawyers experienced in the ramifications of disasters.

What happens after something like the Zeebrugge trial's outcome ... is that the public holds the law in contempt. Rather than use an old system which does not easily fit into the needs of modern-day disasters we need to have a proper look at what is needed and what will work.

That is the opinion of David MacIntosh of Davies Arnold Cooper, a leading firm of solicitors which – significantly – has acted for the defendants in several disaster actions. MacIntosh goes on to say: 'There should be some method of ensuring that corporations as well as individuals who fail in safety responsibility are held accountable, but at present there is no offence which links some safety element with criminal liability.' His own solution, presented at a Law Society conference in October 1991, is embodied in a draft Corporate Accountability Bill. This, if it got on to the statute book through a private member's Bill or by being adopted by the government, would make directors liable to be disqualified for 'misconduct in regard to health and safety' and would require companies to appoint safety auditors, whose reports would appear in the annual report.

Civil courts should be empowered to impose punitive damages, only a portion of which would go to the claimant

---

Other proposals are now emerging. David Tench, legal officer of the Consumers' Association, has suggested the establishment of special disaster courts. Various lawyers, especially those engaged in personal injury litigation, think that civil courts should be empowered to impose punitive damages, only a portion of which would go to the claimant. One possible objection to such measures is that they would reinforce the present tendency for gross negligence or reckless conduct by corporations to be 'decriminalised'. In some cases they might even result in compliance with regulations being used to shield directors and managers from criminal charges.

After much research, reported in a separate publication,[5] the Herald Families Association has recommended the creation of several new offences within the criminal justice system. These would impose a very stringent 'duty of care' on both companies and their senior officers. They would be supported by a series of new, tough sentences for those convicted of criminal misconduct within the area of health and safety. Such penalties would include fines directly related to corporate assets and profits; and 'equity fines' involving the issue of shares into a compensation fund.

The Herald Families Association proposals would allow for individual directors to be prosecuted where they were thought to have shown criminal negligence or recklessness in their own actions, and would allow for the actions of a number of individuals to be aggregated to show that a corporation had failed in its 'duty of care'. Such proposals will not be taken seriously, however, until those responsible for investigating and prosecuting crimes of violence break away from the presumption that disasters, no less than workplace deaths, are invariably accidents because 'nobody intended to harm anyone'.

Many will go on arguing that regulation is better than punishment. This is rather like saying that the most effective way to deal with reckless driving is to put up more speed-restriction signs. At the moment, the impression given – and, to a large extent, the reality – is that the only legislation which really matters to companies is that connected with civil liability. The consequence, according to *The Times*, is that this 'has dulled the edge of moral and legal responsibility, and appeared to reduce safety to the level of being one more commercial factor – as if the only issue was how much of a risk would the undertaking afford to run when measured against consideration of profitability'. The lesson was clear, it said: 'Recklessness by jeopardising public safety should be a crime, whether tragedy ensues or not. And the law should not make it too difficult to prove.'[6]

References

1. Ken Rawson, in paper presented at RINA meeting on 18 April 1989.
2. *Guardian*, 20 October 1990.
3. *Independent on Sunday*, 21 October 1990.
4. *The Times*, 20 October 1990.
5. *Disasters: Where the Law Fails* by David Bergman, Herald Families Association, 1992.
6. *The Times*, 23 June 1989.

CHAPTER THIRTEEN

CORPORATE RESPONSIBILITY: BEYOND THE LAW

'I have always recognised our
corporate responsibility for the loss
of the *Herald*'
– **Jeffrey Sterling.**

'Did you ever expect a corporation
to have a conscience when it
has no soul to be damned and no body to
be kicked?'
– **Edward Thurlow, Lord Chancellor (1731–1806).**

The law can only go so far in making companies act responsibly. Through its regulatory systems it prescribes minimum standards of conduct which help to defend 'good' companies against unfair competition from those intent on putting profit before all other considerations. At a higher level it discourages serious offences by holding out the possibility that the offenders will be severely punished. But there it stops. Beyond the law lies a vast, mostly uncharted area of corporate responsibility. Its only signposts are non-quantifiable concepts such as 'self-regulation', 'ethics', 'good citizenship' and 'values'.

How a company behaves is not wholly determined by the desire to achieve certain profit and growth goals. Other influences include the way society expects it to behave; the image it wishes to present to the outside world, perhaps for purely commercial reasons; and the personal values of the people who own and run it. These things are often in conflict – though apart from the high financial stakes the conflict is probably no greater for a company than for individual members of the community.

Two centuries ago a Lord Chancellor of England, Edward Thurlow, asked: 'Did you ever expect a corporation to have a conscience when it has no soul to be damned and no body to be kicked?' A minority of business leaders still subscribe to that view, though they might hesitate to proclaim it so bluntly. The majority have progressed in their thinking. 'Corporate culture' has become an overworked term in business circles but it has considerable impact on corporate behaviour and, many would insist, on the bottom line.

In the late 1960s and early 1970s there was a surge of interest in the subject of business ethics. Major companies carried out social audits to assess how they were responding (and were perceived to be responding) to current needs and expectations. Many published well-intentioned, though often rather woolly, ethical codes. It did not last. Within a short time most of this activity had been blown off managers' desks by the cold wind of economic recession. There are now signs that the subject is coming back on to corporate agendas, though whether it will prove to be more robust this time round has yet to be demonstrated.

In his book *Capitalism and Freedom,* Milton Friedman gave a very simple definition of the social responsibility of business. It is 'to use its resources and engage in activities designed to increase profits so long as it stays within the rules of the game – which is to say, engaged in open and free competition without deception or fraud'. Unfortunately, recent City scandals have shown how easy it is for the rules of the game to be modified to suit individual interests, and for deception and fraud to be redefined as legitimate tactics.

Sir Adrian Cadbury, chairman of Cadbury-Schweppes, who has master-minded a report on corporate governance, offers a more pragmatic assessment: 'The possibility that ethical and commercial considerations will conflict has always faced those who run companies. It is not a new problem. The difference now is that a more widespread and critical interest is being taken in our decisions and in the ethical judgments which lay behind them.'[1]

The trouble with a subject such as ethics is that it tends to generate the airy-fairy pledges, so clearly divorced from bottom-line realism, that many businessmen find off-putting. There is, however, one responsibility issue which probably does more than any other to relate good intentions to corporate strategy and day-to-day business decisions. This is the responsibility that every company has for the health and safety of three groups of people – its employees, users of its products and services, and members of the community in which it operates. What value is there in a company making a token demonstration of social responsibility by financially supporting efforts to save a distant rain forest if it is simultaneously pumping effluent into a local river? Or in seconding members of its staff to community projects if it is regularly exposing members of the community to avoidable hazards?

The most safety-conscious companies tend to be the most profitable – the link is good management

---

One advantage of focusing on this particular issue is that there is little scope – at least in open discussion – for trade-offs between safety and profitability. No one can seriously dispute the need for all managers to put safety first whenever a conflict arises. Getting managers to do that, however, is more easily said than done. They are not likely to take action systematically unless they personally believe – with the active approval of their superiors – that in the long run higher safety standards will enhance the profitability of the operations for which they are held accountable and will consequently further their own careers.

Richard Warburton, director-general of the Royal Society for the Prevention of Accidents, says: 'More and more companies are taking safety seriously and I would say that the most safety-conscious companies tend to be the most profitable – the common link between these two things is good management.'[2] Safety improvement is more than a debit item in the corporate ledger. There is evidence that it can offer a competitive edge, especially if it is imaginatively presented to the company's customers and other stakeholders.

The other side of that coin is that under-investment in safety almost invariably costs money in the long run. This is dramatically demonstrated when it results in a large number of people being killed or injured. In addition to the direct costs of a disaster there are hidden costs that may bite deep into corporate profits for many years to come. Few will doubt, for instance, that the last nail in the coffin of the ailing US airline Pan-Am was the revelation in the wake of the Lockerbie disaster that its security procedures were inadequate and even penny-pinching. In those circumstances potential customers had no difficulty in relating corporate responsibility to their own well-being.

Before disaster strikes, however, it is only too easy for safety to be overwhelmed by other considerations. The Marine Accident Investigation Branch report on the *Marchioness* sinking identified a preoccupation 'with things rather than people'. It went on to say that the designs of both the riverboat and the dredger which sank it should never have been approved by the Department of Transport. It seems that the safety of passengers had been either overlooked or pushed to one side.

British Rail's plan to become 'business led' was seen by some as a factor in the 1988 Clapham rail disaster. Eleven months before this happened a BR safety director had warned:

> I would not like a major disaster with loss of life to be the reason that forced BR to invest in modern safety aids. There are signs that the past high standards at local level, achieved by giving priority to a 'safe railway' above other items, are starting to be eroded by the change in railway culture ... If continued, this will strike at the root of our culture.[3]

He went on to express concern that safety might not get 'the correct priority' when budgets were set. In one case at least this appears to have happened. A system for automatically stopping trains which passed red lights without permission was not installed by British Rail because managers failed to make a sufficiently attractive case for it. That safety director's warning should be considered in relation to a report by the Railway Inspectorate in December 1991. This included the chilling fact that in the year under review there had been 1,300 signal failures of the type that caused the Clapham disaster.

Buying up companies seemed
a faster, less painful way to grow

With hindsight, the enterprise culture of the 1980s is seen to have been a bit of a sham. Many of its loudly proclaimed benefits have been dissipated by the economic recession that has clouded the start of the present decade. It is tempting, therefore, to suggest that the enterprise culture was also to blame for a noticeable decline in corporate responsibility. While that may be going too far, the 1980s brought four developments that are certainly relevant to the matters being discussed here.

The first of those developments was an outbreak of 'merger mania'. The received wisdom of the day was that in order to survive companies had to get bigger and bigger. Managements then got hooked into a belief that buying up other businesses was a faster and less painful way to grow than developing a company's own markets, physical resources and core skills. Academic research, plus a good deal of hard experience, has demolished that myth. There is very little evidence throughout the world that mergers have ever yielded the synergistic benefits anticipated by their instigators. There is quite a lot of evidence (as in the Ford acquisition of Jaguar) that acquisitions are often ill considered and poorly implemented. It is generally accepted that the failure rate of recent mergers has been as high as 75 per cent.

The second development, also connected with 'merger mania', was the emphasis on short-termism. Fear of being taken over stalked many boardrooms in the 1980s (as it still does). The consequences of that fear have been forcibly described by Sir Anthony Pilkington, chairman of the often pursued but (as yet) never purchased Pilkington Group:

> Concern that a company may be vulnerable to a takeover bid means that management may continually be looking over its shoulder rather than concentrating on the future of the business. Furthermore, management may decide to operate the business for short-term profit, thus neglecting investment which may be necessary for long-term competitiveness.[4]

In those circumstances it is not surprising that corporate responsibility issues, including safety improvement, get less attention than they deserve.

The third significant development in the 1980s was an emasculation of local management. That, too, was a consequence of the new faith in acquisition and diversification. The new folk heroes of the business world were men with little hands-on experience of the activities that had come under their control. Many of them were financial wizards, marketing gurus and entrepreneurs whose reputations were sometimes founded on the short-lived property boom. Some, of course, have survived the change in business conditions and attitudes, but they are increasingly seen as yesterday's men. In future we shall see fewer and fewer of them profiled in the Sunday papers or glorified on the cover of *Time* or *Business Week*.

The fourth development is the erosion of employee loyalty. That, again, is closely related to the other developments. Many thousands of employees, including middle managers, are no longer sure whom they are working for, what they are working for, or even whether there will always be work for them to do. The group directors who formulate strategy – and decide, for example, whether a plant is to be expanded, contracted or wiped out – are far removed from those struggling to hit the profit and growth targets they have set.

It would be wrong to suggest that any of the above developments contributed directly to the Zeebrugge disaster; nevertheless, the changes in the ferry company's ownership most certainly illustrate the difficulties now faced by many enterprises. They also raise one specific question: what exactly is a company taking over, in terms of corporate responsibility, when it buys another? P&O acquired Townsend Thoresen with its parent company European Ferries on 19 January 1987, just six weeks before the capsize of the *Herald of Free Enterprise*. Surely it is unreasonable to hold it responsible, in any way, after such a short period of ownership?

At first sight, there seems to be only one answer. But on further consideration a different picture emerges. In law, P&O was clearly responsible. If the period of ownership had been a single day instead of six weeks it would have made no difference. That was publicly confirmed by Jeffrey Sterling later in 1987. 'I have always recognised our corporate responsibility for the loss of the *Herald*,' he said. 'That was accepted by Townsend Car Ferries ... as parent company P&O has shared the responsibility despite the very short period of ownership ... it is inconceivable that it would have been an "us and them" situation even if that period had been five minutes.'

Townsend, Sterling argued, was a 'very fine company'. He insisted that thousands of its employees were proud of what they had done (clearly referring to the time before March 1987) and were 'devastated' by what was now being said about the company. 'There were certainly no criticisms of its operations in either the industry or the City.'

Bearing in mind Mr Justice Sheen's damning assessment of the quality of Townsend's management – almost without precedent in the findings of technical inquiries – this seems to reflect on Sterling's own assessment of his acquisition. The final comment could also be construed as demonstrating the narrow way in which some members of the shipping industry and the City regard corporate responsibility. 'A very fine company' Townsend may have been. But it was losing money at the time of its acquisition by P&O, and the management standards and operational procedures were well below those that passengers were entitled to expect, as the Sheen inquiry found.

Sterling's comments seem to overlook the fact that a company is the sum of its parts, not simply a highly regarded name. Had P&O examined those management standards and operational procedures more closely in the six weeks before the disaster – or even before the takeover – it might have concluded that Townsend's safety systems were in need of improvement. It would then, one assumes, have suspended operations until the weaknesses had been put right. It was, after all, an assessment by a P&O team that made the company accept responsibility while the Sheen inquiry was still in progress.

Did P&O look at anything other than Townsend's financial and physical assets?

Did P&O look at anything other than Townsend's financial and physical assets? This is an important question for all companies committed to a policy of growth by acquisition. On what information should acquisition decisions be based? In the case of P&O and Townsend there had been links between the two companies which might have alerted someone to the inadequacy of Townsend's safety systems for which responsibility was now being assumed.

P&O, a name revered in maritime circles for over a century and a half, now embraces a number of unrelated businesses. These include Earl's Court and Olympia, Sutcliffe Catering, P&O Vending Services, Buck & Hickman, Bovis Construction, Ashby & Horner and others. While agglomeration does not necessarily put restraints on corporate responsibility, it is liable to create management problems. Group directors and senior executives are unlikely to have had first-hand experience of all, or indeed any, of the enterprises they control. They impose profit and growth targets on their subsidiaries but if day-to-day operations go wrong they can raise their hands and exclaim, 'We didn't know ... the real responsibility lies elsewhere.' Is safety a matter that routinely appears on the agenda of board meetings at P&O and other shipping companies?

Changes in company ownership have an obvious effect on the morale and commitment of a local workforce. Its members realise that the managers they know are no longer making the key decisions. They see their own job security falling into the hands of people who are certainly not swayed by sentiment and may not be capable of appreciating the opportunities for growth or the need for further investment.

In Townsend's case, however, there had been a close relationship with P&O – at least at top management level – for some time before the takeover. At the end of 1984 P&O sold its Anglo-French ferry services to

European Ferries (the owners of Townsend) for £12.5 million. The sale was not welcomed by those who were operating the five vessels in P&O's ferry fleet. They asked for it to be referred to the Monopolies and Mergers Commission (MMC). This request was refused by the then Secretary of State for Trade and Industry, Norman Tebbit.

The next step in the relationship came in December 1985 when P&O bought a 50.1 per cent interest in European Financial Holdings, the company that ran European Ferries' US property investments. This gave P&O 20.8 per cent of European Ferries' shares. As a result Sterling joined the European Ferries board, a position from which he presumably had not only some opportunity to assess the quality of the management of the Townsend Thoresen subsidiary, but also some responsibility for doing so.

In June 1986 P&O announced its intention to bid for the whole of European Ferries. This *was* referred to the MMC, which decided at the end of 1986 that a merger 'does not and may not be expected to operate against the public interest'. Sterling and the European Ferries chairman, Geoffrey Parker, quickly hammered out a deal, and on 19 January 1987 P&O took over European Ferries (which also controlled the ports of Felixstowe and Larne) for £345 million.

The Sunday Times rather oddly referred to it as a 'bloodless coup'. In fact it was, at least in Sterling's eyes, more of a rescue operation. European Ferries had got into difficulties as a result of unwise diversifications following the untimely death of its former chairman, Keith Wickenden, killed in an aircraft accident in July 1983. In the year before its acquisition by P&O the company had lost £1.9 million, compared with a profit of £35.5 million in the preceding year.

The close links between the two companies meant that it could never have been a case of 'us and them', to use Sterling's own phrasing. Through him, they presumably had intimate knowledge of each other's business outlook and values. 'If his opinions were not being heard in the European Ferries boardroom ... then I am much deceived,' observed a business commentator in *The Times* on 4 December 1986.

Jeffrey Sterling began his career as a stockbroker, but soon established a reputation for rejuvenating 'lame ducks'. After 1969, when he assumed control of Sterling Guarantee Trust, he had gone from strength to strength. He joined the P&O board in 1980 and, having won his spurs by defeating an unwelcome takeover bid, became its chairman three years later. In November of that year he outlined his business philosophy to a meeting of more than 70 senior executives from all P&O divisions. 'They will have been left in no doubt that their company has entered a new phase in which tradition will give way, when the chairman decides, to managerial efficiency,' commented *The Times* on 8 November 1983.

Though Sterling does occasionally invoke maritime tradition (he was piped aboard one of his ferries during a long dispute with the NUS), he is essentially an entrepreneur whose personal qualities were recognised during the heady 1980s. A sponsored history of the great shipping company[5] published shortly before the Zeebrugge disaster contains a brief description of his management style: 'He wished to be at the centre of the empire, yet separated from it, together with his closest confidants and support staff, free to survey and control the scene objectively.' It also said that he encouraged 'individual responsibility' and 'displayed an outstanding gift for what can best be described as controlled delegation'.

---

*Business leaders cannot
shrink from their responsibility
to set a moral example*

Delegation, it has been argued, is not simply a matter of pushing decision-making down the line. It is wholly effective only when the corporate values to be observed in making those decisions have been pushed down the line as well. The ability to do this is now regarded as one of the principal responsibilities of top management. 'Business leaders today cannot shrink from their responsibility to set a moral example,' says William C. Butcher, chairman of the Chase Manhattan Corporation. John Akers, chairman of IBM United Kingdom, explains why: 'Ethics and competitiveness are inseparable.'[6]

There is no doubt that many managers are looking for moral leadership at a time when so much media attention is being paid to the regulation of major corporations, some of which appear to have put themselves above the laws governing individual behaviour. In an important study conducted by Columbia Business School in collaboration with Korn/Ferry International, the world's largest firm of executive headhunters, 1,400 senior managers in 14 countries were asked to rank the personal qualities they thought would be required of the ideal chief executive officer in the year 2000. They put high ethical standards at the top of their list. Chief executive officers of the next century would have to be 'above reproach'. Their own ethical standards would be indispensable in establishing the company's external credibility, in setting internal standards of conduct, and in 'keeping the organisation out of the courts'.[7]

That final benefit shows greater realism than was often attached to corporate responsibility in the past. The 'ethics' movement of the early 1970s failed to win a permanent place in management thinking because it treated social responsibility as a separate issue – the gift-wrapping on a profit-oriented package. As such, it was bound to be discarded when the going got rough.

Attitudes are now much more realistic. At an international management conference in 1990 Dr Peter F. Mueller, a former ITT executive running a consultancy called Business & Ethics, gave three main reasons why companies were becoming increasingly concerned with their social responsibilities. The first is the rapid growth of external pressures, particularly on environmental issues. The second is the realisation that unless business puts its own house in order it can expect tougher regulation by both national governments and the European Commission. The third is that in the minds of employees social values are taking the place of traditional virtues like hard work.

Expanding on the third reason, Mueller suggested that ethics could be 'very instrumental in building company loyalty and team spirit'. That is clearly an important motivation at a time when employers throughout Europe are finding it increasingly difficult to recruit the highly skilled workers they need to meet the challenges of global competition. The 'yuppy' era is over: today's high-fliers are looking for some kind of social value in what they do for a living. The company with a 'responsible' image has a definite advantage when it comes to replenishing and reinforcing its managerial strength.

Consumers, too, are beginning to look for something more than quick service and low prices. The 'green' revolution may at times seem misdirected, even driven by commercial interests, but is having a lasting effect on buying patterns. That is why so many companies are switching their advertising thrust from brand promotion to the promotion of corporate values.

One of the world's most respected management thinkers, Professor Rosabeth Moss Kanter of Harvard Business School, believes that corporate values are a 'genuine competitive advantage ... an enduring factor amid so many changes in products and services ... a means of changing from a roadblock organisation to a flexible organisation capable of working across national boundaries.'[8]

*Values give guidance and motivation
in situations where the rulebook ceases
to be effective*

In a world where responsibility for business decisions is being decentralised and employees empowered to take more decisions on their own initiative, values 'act as corporate glue', says Moss Kanter. They give guidance and motivation in situations where the rulebook ceases to be effective. They also help to eradicate the 'cowboy managers' intent on protecting their own interests rather than their company's interests.

The health and safety issue shows that genuine corporate responsibility is an area beyond regulation. As Adam Smith said in a less demanding age: 'Without this sacred regard for the general rules of morality there is no man whose conduct can be much depended upon.' The same is unquestionably true of corporate conduct. If any good is to emerge from the recent series of disasters it is that managers are becoming more aware of that fact.

There is still one unanswered question: where does personal responsibility begin and end? In earlier decades it was generally assumed that the man at the top would resign if the operations under his control went seriously wrong. That no longer holds good. 'I take full responsibility' so often means 'I take nominal responsibility but it's not real responsibility because I relied on people down the line and they let me down.' It is an understandable attitude but not one that, in either the public or private sector, is going to do anything to prevent further disasters.

Sadly, the failure of the Zeebrugge corporate manslaughter trial seemed to condone an all-too-prevalent attitude among senior managers: 'Don't tell me what is going on because if I know, I might be held accountable'.

References

1. *Harvard Business Review*, September/October 1987.
2. *The Financial Times*, 8 November 1989.
3. *The Financial Times*, 27 July 1989.
4. *The Times*, 18 April 1991.
5. *The Story of P&O*, Weidenfeld & Nicholson, 1986.
6. Speech at New Orleans, 15 May 1987.
7. *Reinventing the CEO*. A global study conducted in 1988/9 by Korn/Ferry International and Columbia University School of Business.
8. Speech at the 23rd International Human Resources Management Conference, Barcelona.

CHAPTER FOURTEEN

THE ROLE OF GOVERNMENT

'The *Herald* disaster showed us that it is
in fact the most obvious things that can
sometimes be overlooked by the law'
– Lord Brabazon, Minister for Aviation and Shipping.

'To sit in the Cabinet room taking part in conversation,
of course there is a sense of being in the corridors
of power. Of course, it is exciting.'
– Jeffrey Sterling.

The governmental role in passenger transport is inevitably complex. One of its two main agencies, the Department of Transport, presides over a multi-faceted, widely dispersed operation involving a huge number of private carriers and one mammoth organisation – British Rail – which has yet to be privatised. With the growth of international transport, its dealings with regulatory bodies in other countries have become increasingly complex. There is clearly an obligation on the part of the department to ensure that all carriers do everything they reasonably can to avoid harming passengers, other members of the public, and the environment. It has to anticipate what could go wrong, legislate for this, and then ensure that everybody abides by its regulations. If something does go wrong it has a duty to try to ensure that the same mistakes are never made again. At the same time it is expected to avoid over-regulation, which would impede fair competition.

The fact that privately owned carriers use highways, rivers and seaways controlled by public bodies leads to some confusion over responsibility and accountability. Planners sometimes seem to overlook the safety implications of this. For instance, it has been proposed that British Rail should sell the use of its tracks to private operators. If there is a crash, who will be held accountable? And who will have had the prime responsibility for preventing that crash?

The Department of Transport has, not surprisingly, found itself at the centre of several of Britain's recent disasters. It has not always emerged with credit. The main criticism that can be levelled at it is that in making regulations – and then seeing they are periodically reviewed and updated where necessary – it is almost invariably reactive rather than proactive. In the months following a disaster we get a clutch of new regulations most people would have assumed were already in place. There is great danger in lack of foresight. Regulations ought to be viewed as minimum standards – a safety net to catch the relatively few rogue operators who are prepared, given the chance, to put profits before lives. Progressive carriers are expected to improve on these minima in the light of their own operating experience and sense of corporate responsibility. Regrettably, this does not always happen. The result is that when things go wrong, the department's lack of foresight becomes an excuse and, if needed, a legal defence.

Mr Justice Sheen, in his report on the Zeebrugge disaster, pointed to one effect of this.

> The responsibilities of the Department for matters of safety of life at sea are very wide. After a casualty has occurred there is a natural instinct on the part of shipowners to adopt the attitude that they had not taken certain precautions because the Department had not made rules which required those precautions. From that defensive position there can easily develop what appears to the public, probably erroneously, to be a cover-up.

Whatever weight should be put on that word 'probably', Zeebrugge provided a classic example of too little governmental intervention too late. 'If it is the view of Parliament that the taking to sea of a ro-ro ferry with her bow or stern doors open ought to be a criminal offence, then Parliament must enact the appropriate legislation,' said Sheen. Parliament did so. Regulations insisting on bow door indicator lights were introduced, together with a dozen or so other measures identified – if identification were really needed – by the disaster. This enabled the then Transport Secretary, Paul Channon, to preen himself on the department's rapid response. He seemed unaware that what public safety calls for is not response but anticipation.

There was a similarly quick response to the *Marchioness* disaster in the River Thames. By the end of the month, new safety regulations were issued for the river. The sad paradox is that when it acts as quickly as this the government virtually confirms suspicions that regulations were simply not tight enough. The regulatory changes produced by Zeebrugge provoked one MP to ask the Secretary of State for Transport the pointed question: 'Is my Right Honourable Friend saying that it is not a statutory offence to take to sea a ship that is unseaworthy, but he proposes to legislate to make it so?' In fact, this was a pretty accurate assessment of the minister's comments.

The Department of Transport exists in a political wilderness

In the case of the *Herald*, more extreme changes in the safety practices and fundamental design of ro-ros were slow in emerging. It was 1990 before the results of government-sponsored research became known. Significant improvements in stability (by retrospectively applying the SOLAS 90 standards) were not under way at the end of 1992, and there was still disagreement over when this work would start and finish. It was then five and a half years since the *Herald* had dramatically identified the need for such action. A similarly reactive rather than proactive approach was taken in the case of the *Titanic*. It was discovered, after the event, that there were no rules insisting that there was space in a ship's lifeboats for everyone on board a ship. There were 2,201 people on board the *Titanic* and room for 1,178 in the lifeboats. Legislation had failed to take account of the increased size of modern ships.

Lord Brabazon, Minister for Aviation and Shipping, made a telling comment when discussing the Merchant Shipping Bill in the House of Lords. 'The *Herald* disaster showed us that it is in fact the most obvious things that can sometimes be overlooked by the law,' he said. In other professions and occupations people are reprimanded, punished or dismissed for ignoring the obvious. Brabazon appeared to regard it as a natural phenomenon. The weight of evidence on ro-ro stability and the fierce competitiveness of the cross-Channel market might have alerted the department to these 'obvious things'. They did not.

One possible explanation for this omission lies in the perpetual reorganisation a variety of governments has carried out within maritime research groups. The National Maritime Institute was established in 1976. In 1982 it became the NMI, which then merged with the British Ship Research Association in 1985 to become British Maritime Technology (BMT), itself a privatised version of the ship research division of the

National Physical Laboratory. So much change is hardly likely to breed confidence or consistency.

The reorganisation brought no additional finance – despite well-publicised concerns about ro-ro stability and other hazards. One month after Zeebrugge, a BMT spokesman admitted: 'We now have to be both super-efficient and super-committed to do basic research.'[1]

The Department of Transport exists in something of a political wilderness. The post of Transport Secretary is not one of the most coveted offices of state, burdened as it is with large and apparently insoluble problems such as traffic congestion and the minutiae of regulation and legislation. Until the recent emergence of environmental issues, transport has not been regarded as a vote-winner. In the 1987 Conservative Party manifesto, it was given less space than the arts and there was little change five years later. The degree of importance attached to it is reflected in the long list of ministers who have had the portfolio. In the 1980s, Nicholas Ridley, John Moore, Paul Channon and Cecil Parkinson all for a time held the post; since then Malcolm Rifkind and John McGregor have done so. The Department's turnover at the top is matched only by that of the DTI.

Lean, fit, a vital national asset

The relationship between the Department of Transport and companies in the transport industry is necessarily close, perhaps uniquely so. This can give an impression of complacency. In 1990, for example, a report on the state of the merchant shipping industry was published by the government and the industry itself. The committee was chaired by Jeffrey Sterling and Transport Secretary Cecil Parkinson. It concluded that the industry was 'lean, fit, a vital national asset, and well placed to take advantage of the growth in world trade'. Such optimism seemed to ignore the fact that Britain's registered mainland merchant fleet had declined from 1,275 to 381 between 1980 and 1989 and the number of seafarers from 61,000 to 21,000.

There are other, more controversial, examples of weaknesses resulting from the close relationship between government and the shipping industry. In 1980 the 90,000-ton MV *Derbyshire* disappeared with all hands in the South China Sea. It was assumed it had been hit by a typhoon. Forty-four people died on the *Derbyshire* and more were lost when a sister ship sank in similar circumstances. When the ship's builder, Swan Hunter, was being privatised in 1985, the government promised to indemnify any future management against litigation arising out of the ship's loss. This may have been seen as a sensible move in order to make Swan Hunter a more attractive commercial proposition. Shadow Transport Secretary John Prescott commented: 'The Government had a direct financial interest in ensuring its inquiry reports were non-committal as to why the *Derbyshire* sank. It is all a damning indictment of the priority we give to the loss of capital compared to the loss of life.'[2]

To the ferry companies, their relationship with the department is of utmost importance. Any change in policy – such as supporting rail transport at the expense of cars – has a huge impact in terms of both employment and finance. Political decisions such as Mrs Thatcher's shrewd move in privatising Sealink before announcing the Channel tunnel project, can greatly affect profits. The government's response to Zeebrugge drew heavily on representatives from shipping interests. Research commissioned by the Department of Transport into ro-ro stability was partly carried out by a wholly owned subsidiary of P&O, Three Quays. A Sealink subsidiary was also involved in it.

'Ministers represent P&O'

In 1988 the Department of Transport set up a working party into the installation of draught gauges on ro-ros, a Sheen recommendation, after the GCBS had objected to its initial suggestions. The working party involved three representatives of the department as well as Leslie Stephenson, assistant managing director of P&O European Ferries; George Williamson from a P&O subsidiary; Tony Rogan from Hart Fenton, a Sealink subsidiary; and Walter Welch, director of the Marine Division of the GCBS. The representatives of the ship operators outnumbered government officials and there were no independent members.

The relationship between P&O and government has been frequently commented on and analysed. It led Tony Benn to observe in the House of Commons in May 1988 that 'ministers represent P&O'. An over-the-top comment without doubt – but one that in some ways reflected the public concern engendered by the Zeebrugge revelations and, in particular, by the efforts of P&O's chairman to distance shore management from the causes of the disaster.

Commentators focused on three aspects of the relationship: the company's generous financial support for the Conservative Party, the influence undoubtedly wielded by Sterling in an unpaid government post, and the company's aggressive lobbying on behalf of both itself and the UK shipping industry.

Impropriety was not alleged but there were accusations that P&O was sometimes heavy-handed in its efforts to win favourable consideration.

This element of the Zeebrugge story – coloured, perhaps, by the unusual circumstance that the company was then facing a serious criminal charge – raises issues of much wider significance. How, where and when does interaction between public servants and private enterprises go beyond what is deemed to be socially acceptable, rather than just legally permissible? Take political lobbying, a business activity which has grown more intense and sophisticated in recent years. It is clear that companies, and indeed individuals, have a right to 'put a case' to the politicians and bureaucrats whose decisions directly affect their fortunes. The politicians and bureaucrats, for their part, have a duty to listen and, where appropriate, take account of what they hear. But when does 'putting a case' become an attempt to win unfair consideration, the use of corporate muscle to override more legitimate interests?

The lines of 'acceptability' are ill-defined. They are, moreover, constantly changing, along with social values and expectations. What was deemed acceptable in past years may rightly be frowned upon today. There is also the question of maintaining public confidence. That, surely, merits close attention by all the parties concerned at a time when politicians are proclaiming the virtues of 'open government' and citizen's rights', when public confidence in the probity of business has been dented by the Robert Maxwell and other scandals, and when the performance of regulatory bodies is being scrutinised more critically than ever before.

In fairness, it must be pointed out that some of the lobbying activities for which P&O has been criticised since the Zeebrugge disaster have failed completely and have even had a negative effect by attracting that criticism.

The Conservative Party is undoubtedly financially indebted to P&O. Under Sterling, the company's donations have increased substantially. In 1984 it gave £20,000 and in 1987, the year of the Zeebrugge disaster, it gave £100,000 – then the largest ever corporate donation to a political party and treble the previous year's figure. In 1989 it donated a further £100,000, the third largest contribution (after Taylor Woodrow's £150,000 and United Biscuits' £106,000).

Explaining why companies donate money to the Conservative Party, its former chairman, Norman Tebbit, said: 'They donate money for the purpose of securing a government and a climate which is favourable to business in general. They're not buying favours for their company.' Others are more cynical, or perhaps more realistic. In 1991 the British Airways chairman Lord King announced the company would not be making its usual annual donation to the Conservative Party. In the previous year it had given £40,000. 'In view of the decisions by the Government ... no further political contributions will be made in the current financial year,' said King. He was referring to the government's decision to take away four of BA's slots to Tokyo and open up Heathrow Airport to other airlines. The link in his mind between governmental decision-making and the political donation was made clear.

'A text-book Thatcherite entrepreneur'

P&O's strongest link with the government is through Jeffrey Sterling. One of the many profiles of Sterling observed that he is 'most comfortable in City banking parlours and cosy conversations at Number 10'. Being close to the centre of power is obviously something which appeals to Sterling, 'To sit in the Cabinet room taking part in conversation, of course there is a sense of being in the corridors of power. Of course, it is exciting,' he has said.[3] He was once labelled 'Mrs Thatcher's favourite businessman'. From 1982 until 1990, Sterling was an unpaid adviser to the DTI. First recruited by the then Secretary of State Patrick Jenkin, he served under six subsequent ministers: Cecil Parkinson, Norman Tebbit, Leon Brittan, Paul Channon, Lord Young and Nicholas Ridley. Of these, Parkinson, Channon and Ridley also served the government as Secretaries of Transport.

In 1988, replying to a letter from the Herald Families Association expressing dismay that Sterling did not elect to step down while one of his subsidiaries was the subject of a criminal investigation, one of the Prime Minister's private secretaries naively insisted that Sterling could not be accused of self-interest because his government post was unpaid.

Sterling was no stranger to the importance of political connections. Despite being, in the words of one commentator, 'a textbook Thatcherite entrepreneur', he is not afraid of doing business with Labour or Conservative. He was made a director of British Airways in 1979 by then Trade

Minister John Smith. And, when Sterling eventually relinquished his DTI post in 1990, he immediately began to campaign for tax concessions for the shipping industry, which hardly seemed in the true spirit of a free enterprise culture driven by market forces.

The nature of Sterling's work with the DTI remained, to a large extent, unexplained. 'I was not a politician, nor a political adviser; my answers were always from a commonsensical point of view,' he once said.[4] His role did, however, demand a secretary at the DTI and a direct telephone link to the Minister. Early in the relationship, one observer noted: 'There are three kinds of outsider adviser to government: people who write speeches; people who get asked for their opinion, and Jeffrey Sterling and David Young.'

Young went on to take charge of the DTI, converting it into the 'Department for Enterprise'. He retained Sterling's services. They had been friends since Sterling's City days. Of Sterling's involvement with the DTI, Young said: 'He's a leading businessman who knows what is commercially realistic. Jeffrey must take a great deal of credit for a number of the decisions taken by the DTI during the last few years.'

The private secretary to the Prime Minister said, by way of explanation: 'Sir Jeffrey Sterling supplies advice to the Government from time to time on the basis of his specialist expertise.' One politician he worked with observed: 'He's not a man for great policy thinking, but he's very adept at producing information and ideas.'[5]

Sterling's work was broad ranging. In his biography, Young wrote: 'Jeffrey served as special adviser with distinction for many years. He was never a full-time adviser, his work precluded that, but worked on particular projects.' These included the privatisation of British Telecom, the Airbus, and even broadcasting. He was also involved in the later stages of British Aerospace's purchase of Rover.

Sterling clearly had access to the highest levels of government. 'He is very special, very powerful ... in this (unpaid) job ... he is astonishingly close to government and to documents and sensitive information,' said *The Sunday Times* on 8 May 1988.

Government spokesmen were quick, however, to make it clear that Sterling's work did not compromise the work of the DTI. Sir Brian Hayes, a former permanent secretary at that department, commented: 'Of course the DTI has to deal with questions which affect P&O, particularly in the competition field. But when that happens Jeffrey is cut out of all the circuits. He doesn't see any of the papers.'

Government ministers and the bureaucrats who serve them all too rarely have hands-on experience of business. In a free-market economy it is desirable that they should be prepared to take advice from those who have – especially those who have demonstrated that they measure up to world standards of company direction and management. But any interaction between public and commercial interests, whether formal or informal, holds certain dangers.

The rules of the game are not written down. Perhaps they never will be. Nevertheless, the underlying principles need to be re-examined and discussed more openly. Some of the questions raised by the Zeebrugge disaster and its aftermath may help to accelerate that process.

References

1. *New Scientist*, 2 April 1987.
2. *The Independent*, 29 June 1990.
3. *The Times*, 2 March 1991.
4. Ibid.
5. *The Daily Telegraph*, 27 April 1988.

CHAPTER FIFTEEN

THE WORLD BEYOND

Every disaster provokes a response of outrage from politicians, experts, concerned parties and the public at large. As the disaster disappears from the headlines, so usually does the missionary zeal for change. Any disaster, however large, is quickly consigned to yesterday's news and causes. Inquests and inquiries briefly arouse passions again, but politicians and those who could investigate change are all too often covering their tracks and moving on to the next big issue.

Lessons are not automatically learned. People get on with their lives assuming that things have changed, improvements have been made. It is not necessarily true. The loss of 193 lives in the Zeebrugge disaster produced a sadly predictable response. The mistakes made on 6 March 1987 and in the months and years subsequent to the disaster have not all been learned from. Indeed, many of the crucial issues for managers and companies are only now creeping on to the agenda. Five years after the Zeebrugge disaster, it is time to take stock of what has been achieved and of the many changes required not only to make ferry travel safer but to make managers and companies in all industries more responsible for their actions.

The profit motive

There is little evidence to suggest that short-term thinking has been eradicated from the boardrooms of Britain. Yet, says Kenneth Andrews, author of *Ethics in Practice*: 'Management's total loyalty to the maximisation of profit is the principal obstacle to achieving higher standards of ethical practice.'[1]

While Western business has learned a lot from the Japanese way of doing things, it has conspicuously failed to acknowledge one of the fundamentals of Japanese economic and commercial success: long-term thinking and planning. Managers from all areas of the business world have advocated an increase in long-term thinking. Every year the Institute of Directors meets and bemoans short-termism. Yet little happens to change the pressure on business people to produce annual dividends for shareholders. The emphasis on producing yearly and half-yearly figures brings with it the media glare of annual general meetings and pressure on managers to produce impressive results.

Two American lawyers, Martin Lipton and Steven Rosenblum, have challenged the entire system. They suggest that instead of an annual judgement on managerial and corporate performance, there should be a meeting every five years. At each meeting, directors would put themselves up for re-election on the strength of a detailed account of their performance over the previous five years and their plans for the next five. An independent investment bank or consulting company would carry out an appraisal of the company's plans and performance. In an interesting adjunct to this process, the two suggest that takeovers should be considered only at the five-yearly meeting, to protect companies from continually fighting off hostile bids.

These suggestions are extreme. They do, however, point to the need for fundamental changes in attitude so that management thinking is no longer inextricably tied to reporting and pursuing success on a yearly basis. Thinking must change if methods of reporting are also to change.

Such ideas are given little support by those who make a living from the existing system or by companies which have grown through acquisition. Yet the case of P&O's acquisition of Townsend Thoresen provided a textbook example of a takeover which added up on paper, but would have presented a somewhat different picture if a closer look had been taken at managerial systems and standards of operation. The continuing fascination for takeovers rather than organic growth will doubtless lead to other examples of takeovers where the profit motive overcomes more stringent examination of a company's activities. This is clearly unhealthy for the future success of companies and potentially dangerous for the safety and well-being of customers.

If change is to come, shareholders are likely to play a pivotal role in achieving it. They, and institutional investors in particular, must take an interest in the activities of the company they own a share of. This is already supported by the Association of British Insurers, which represents a large number of institutional investors.

Developing this point, Jonathan Clarkham (a senior adviser to the Governor of the Bank of England) has urged shareholders to combine to bring increased pressure to bear on companies with poor management, rather than relying on market forces – in the shape of takeover bids – to bring about restructuring. He says:

> If it gets to the point where a takeover bid is made, our system has already failed. Any system fails occasionally. Ours is failing consistently because it has that systematic weakness – that there is no way of ensuring that boards are up to the mark if the shareholders opt out.[2]

According to Jeffrey Sterling, closer involvement by shareholders encourages long-term thinking. He says:

> Ownership generates and encourages commitment – to the future of the company, to its customers and to its workforce. In turn, this generates a stability which helps these companies think and act more strategically. Companies do need a long-term strategy to ensure long-term profitability and growth.[3]

Shareholders and, in particular, institutional investors have an important part to play in changing the attitudes of business people. There are some signs that shareholders are acting more responsibly. Small investors are, for example, joining together at annual general meetings to ensure that their voice is heard. Bodies representing institutional investors are also increasingly quick to claim that they are interested in long-term prosperity. The truth is that shareholders have little impact on the way a company is run. Annual general meetings stifle rather than encourage debate. There are no other platforms for shareholders to voice their feelings. Though they own the companies, they are unrepresented on boards. This gives them ownership without responsibility, and allows the management to do what it sees fit.

For true corporate responsibility to be achieved, the divide between shareholders and management needs to be narrowed. Shareholders should act as owners and managers should be responsive to their opinions on the direction the company is taking. Both ought to be more dedicated to long-term growth and profitability than to the short-term attraction of increasing dividends.

Design

Zeebrugge proved that it is unacceptable, in any business, to wait for the product or machine to go wrong before taking action. The addition of simple indicator lights would have told the captain whether the bow doors were shut. More fundamentally, bulkheads would have slowed the vessel's capsize. The evidence for the importance of these design modifications was well documented, though not insisted on in law. P&O's declared policy has been to comply with the standards laid down by current legislation. But every company ought to do everything in its power to protect the lives of customers and employees. It is both a moral and a commercial essential. No company should sit down and wait for the government or other regulatory bodies to make it act once a risk has been identified.

The role and responsibility of designers has now broadened. 'Few designers can now regard their role to be simply the satisfaction of their clients' requirements just within the law,' says RINA's Professor Ken Rawson.[4] Their brief must now encompass some degree of responsibility for the end-result of their work. In the first instance, it is the designer who must take responsibility for safety. Doubts need to be voiced publicly, not simply in professional magazines, and action needs to be taken. Such responsibility spreads to all involved in the design process. Viscount Caldecote and Alex Moulton of the RINA said in 1987:

> If our profession of engineering is to be highly regarded, every engineer involved in design must be prepared to refuse to be associated with a design which is not fully fit for its specified task, particularly in regard to its reliability, its life and most of all its safety.[5]

As poignantly demonstrated in the Zeebrugge case, within companies the design function has been historically undervalued and isolated. To be truly effective and responsive, it has to be closely integrated and linked to overall strategy. Those in charge of design should have a clear mandate for action. Their work should not be restricted to new products, but they should be constantly improving and enhancing the design capabilities of existing ones. At Townsend, design input seemed to come to an end once new ships were in operation. The design function was isolated – actually inland – and did not carry the necessary power to effect change. Such isolation from the mainstream of a company's activities has clear repercussions. Operating procedures are likely to expose frailties in the design that are not communicated to the designers. The company is unlikely to be involved in the wider design debate, the innovative thinking which improves and enhances product performance and safety.

The overall design lesson of the Zeebrugge disaster is that no product, however large, however costly, exists in a vacuum. Its efficiency has continually to be reassessed in the light of changes in operational requirements and in the behaviour of those using it. This is also true of the product's safety factors. At the lowest level designers have a duty to 'stay with' their designs for as long as these are in use. At a higher level they should seize opportunities to demonstrate that design innovations in safety, no less than in other operational factors, can provide a company with a genuine competitive advantage.

Safety

Unquestionably, a lot has been done to increase safety standards on cross-Channel ferries. Many of the recommendations of the Sheen inquiry have also been implemented. Basic requirements – such as bridge indicator lights – are now law. On board ship, passengers are made more aware of safety procedures than they were. Nevertheless it is a fact that only a few of the ferries carrying passengers to and from UK ports in 1992 satisfy the SOLAS 90 standard of damage stability (that is, stability after damage or flooding) which the Department of Transport now believes is necessary to reduce the possibility of rapid capsize. And it is likely to be at least 2005 before all of them do so – 18 years after the bitter lessons of Zeebrugge were made public.

Ferry operators repeatedly claim that they are 'dedicated to safety'. All this usually means is that they have satisfied whatever regulations have been forced upon them by bodies whose track record is one of belated response rather than foresight. In the 1990s that kind of 'minimum conformance' is not enough. Companies which claim to be pace-setters in other areas ought not to have to be legislated into making changes such as those shown to be necessary by disasters like Zeebrugge. If they really want the public to believe that for them 'safety is paramount' they should look up 'paramount' in a dictionary – and then act on what they find.

A system of licensing for ships and operators was called for by the

NUS at the Sheen inquiry. The NUS lawyer said that if Townsend had been working to a similar system to that used by airlines it was 'a reasonable prediction that any licence it held to operate vessels would be withdrawn'. This practical suggestion was rejected by the government. None of the five post-Zeebrugge Transport Secretaries has explained why.

In general terms, the capsize of the *Herald* demonstrated the need for strong and consistent managerial involvement in all aspects of safety. Responsibility for safety must be taken (and be seen to be taken) by the board of directors. In the case of Townsend, managerial responsibility for safety was unstructured and vague. Since Zeebrugge, the company has accepted that safety demands commitment at a senior level and a board director has been assigned overall control of safety. A stable door has been shut.

Part of this managerial responsibility must be to ensure that the importance of safety, and everyone's involvement in maintaining high safety levels, must be regularly and clearly communicated. Safety policy needs to be clearly understood and people's understanding of it monitored. Communication, and its impact on safety, was a crucial aspect of the Zeebrugge disaster. It showed that:

1. Human fallibility has to be accepted and systems developed which minimise the risk of human error. Townsend's systems simply failed to acknowledge the likelihood of human error. They also failed to identify the areas and procedures intrinsic to effective safety. Crucial areas – such as shutting the bow doors – should have fail-safe systems to back them up.

2. Safety procedures themselves need to be regularly monitored, added to and improved. Monitoring and reviews must be acted on. Lessons must be learned when things go wrong. Companies should conduct regular safety reviews analysing potential problems. The systems operated by Townsend had stood the test of time, but little else. Any rigorous examination of them would have indicated that they were obviously flawed and with each additional voyage the company's luck – and that of its customers – was in greater danger of running out.

3. Procedures need to be appropriate for the hardware and written for the specific application. (In the case of the *Herald*, procedures were 'lifted' from other ferries with visor bow doors, ignoring the fundamental difference of a ferry with clam doors.)

4. Standing orders should be clear and practical, drawn up using the experience and knowledge of all those involved. They should be both authoritative and flexible enough to meet the individual needs of a division or particular business operation.
5. In operational matters of importance there should be a positive reporting system. That is a concept which can be implemented with 100 per cent reliability through even the most elementary communication channels.
6. Suggestions and concerns about safety should be acted on and taken seriously. Mistakes should not be a matter of regret, but of action.

Zeebrugge also showed that safety procedures should bear *both* customers and employees in mind. Customers should be well informed and reassured. They should not be blasé about safety, believing it to be the sole preserve of the company. They have an active role to play – communicating that message, however, must be the responsibility of the company.

Safety procedures on ferries did not bear the paying customers in mind. The research by the Consumers' Association highlighted the difficulties passengers would face in the event of an emergency. Companies must consider what it feels like to be a customer. These were the observations of a passenger who travelled on a ferry shortly after Zeebrugge:

> The bars and lounges were over-crowded with passengers sitting in every available space. Trying to escape in an emergency would have been impossible. There still seems to be no limit to the number of passengers allowed on board and no passenger list. Safety procedures are not mentioned as, for example, in planes. Just looking for the duty-free shop is confusing enough let alone searching for emergency exits in a panic.

Such safety issues, and the legitimate concerns of passengers, can only be fully understood if managers actually use their own products and services and seek out the experiences, fears and concerns of customers. If companies ignore the well-being of their own customers, the customers will eventually shun them.

People

The way in which P&O and Townsend treated their employees provided important insights into their general approach to management. A number of important factors emerged with general implications.

1. Working hours and systems should be responsive to individual situations. If they are laid down centrally with little input from employees or line managers, they run the risk of being operationally dangerous or inefficient. Here, and throughout a business, managers need to be aware of what actually happens, how their decisions are put into practice. Through monitoring they should be able to spot difficulties and inefficiencies and then solve them.
2. In jobs where teamwork is a vital ingredient, it should be encouraged through stability of personnel and regular team meetings. Changes of rota, crews and personnel on the *Herald* meant that teamwork simply could not be developed.
3. There should be an avenue for complaints about personnel procedures and they should be taken seriously when made. Concern about job descriptions, for example, was disregarded – allowing them to evolve was no substitute for organisation.

    The last person to leave the car deck on the night of the disaster didn't check the doors were closed or close them himself. 'He took a narrow view of his duties and it is most unfortunate that he took this attitude,' commented Sheen.

    There is a delicate balance between giving too much freedom (seen in the case of Townsend directors) and allowing people to stick rigidly to tightly defined job descriptions.
4. Increasing the number of hours worked does not increase the quality of work completed. Similarly, any decrease in manning levels needs to be clearly explained to employees and customers alike.

Communications

The *Herald* disaster poignantly demonstrated the need for employees to exercise their own responsibilities. Managers ignored the worries of employees. If employees think something is important enough, and if it affects something as fundamental as safety, they have a responsibility to express their views.

Strangely in a free society, there is little protection for employees who see something fundamentally wrong or dangerous and then tell others. If this continues, companies will be allowed to become even more secretive and employees will become even less powerful.

The communications issues raised by Zeebrugge also had external dimensions. It is clear that communications, particularly in a crisis, now form a substantial part of the skills expected by managers. A survey of the Times Top 1,000 companies showed that 63 per cent agreed a crisis is as inevitable as death or taxes. In another survey only 24 per cent of chief executives said they had training in crisis management. Over 91 per cent thought their firm was vulnerable to an external crisis.[6] Significantly, in one survey 42 per cent of chief executives said that the crises they faced were due to poor management.[7]

The truth of the 1990s – and doubtless of the future – is that people are more likely to believe the media than the viewpoint, however valid and accurate, of a faceless manager they have never seen before. P&O's public relations fiascos demonstrated the importance of having managers who are skilled at using the media. Their inability to collect and communicate vital information was a telling reflection on their training, sensitivity and knowledge of the business they purported to manage.

Government

The importance of transport as a vote-winner is increasing. Concern for the environment and calls for improved public transport have seen to that. There is little consistency. Rail services, for example, were all but ignored in the 1980s. Now, they are gaining more attention. Even so, there is a lack of independence in much of the work of the Department of Transport and its regulatory bodies. Only by giving these bodies significant independent powers will the ability of legislators be able to match the onward progress of technological improvement.

When it comes to the ferry industry, the government's responsibility is clear. 'Commercial expediency cannot be given as an excuse to absolve governments of their responsibility to the public to ensure that passenger ro-ro ferries do not capsize following an incident, before the passengers have a reasonable chance to evacuate the ship,' says the Nautical Institute.

Governments will only fully realise their responsibility when safety becomes a vote-winning issue. Until then their ability to act in advance of the next disaster must continue to be questioned.

Management and corporate responsibility

'Business decisions are like stones thrown into a pool, which is society, and companies are asked to take account of the ripples they cause,' says Sir Adrian Cadbury. Managers and companies must increasingly be aware of the broader implications of their decisions. It is clear that, after the entrepreneurial fervour of the 1980s, society's expectations of managers and companies are changing. The manager of the future will have to be aware of ethical issues and manage in an ethical way. Already business schools are incorporating courses on business ethics and responsibility into their MBA programmes. It is a slow process of learning, backed by even slower changes in the law which make managers and companies more accountable. It mirrors a trend in society – away from irresponsible money-making to more conservative, sustainable and responsible ways of doing business. The ability of managers to move with the times and shake off the excesses of recent years will form one of the cornerstones of a more responsible society.

One evening does not make a disaster. For the survivors and the bereaved there are, even now, years of suffering and torment ahead. Friday 6 March 1987 was only the start of a lengthy period of grief, readjustment and, for some, guilt. 'I would not like anyone to suffer what myself and my family have suffered. It was a very traumatic experience which destroyed our lives,' says Andrew Parker, one of the civilian heroes of the disaster.

'I shall always carry the guilt. It is not up to me to blame anyone else and I am not going to,' said assistant bosun, Mark Stanley. Others are in a similar position – constantly reminded of their part in the disaster.

For the families affected by Zeebrugge, the intervening years have been very painful. Some have channelled their energies into the Herald Families Association. This group came together at the end of 1987 to help people to give one another mutual support and work positively for change. Its aims are to assist families in coming to terms with the disaster;

seek justice for them; provide information; and do something positive to ensure such a tragedy does not happen again.

'The initial reaction of the living victims of disasters is invariably a mixture of grief, frustration and anger,' says Peter Spooner, who has been active in the association since its inception.

> Grief needs neither explanation or justification. The frustration comes from the difficulties we encounter in trying to find out what is happening. Anger is generated by many things. One of these is the reluctance of the authorities to hold anyone accountable for anything. Another is that the law – and by implication society – invariably seems to place a lower value on human life than on property. The anger is compounded by an almost paranoic suspicion that powerful forces are conspiring to cover things up.

For some of those concerned, the memory of Zeebrugge does not cast such a long shadow. P&O has gone from strength to strength. In 1991 its ferries carried more than 12 million passengers and a record 2.2 million tourist vehicles, and the group made a pre-tax profit of £217.4 million on a turnover of nearly £5 billion. For Jeffrey Sterling, the Zeebrugge tragedy has not acted as an impediment to an already high-flying business career. His role in government continued until early in 1990. He was made a life peer in Mrs Thatcher's resignation honours list.

The words 'business as usual' can be a threat to survival rather than a rallying cry. In the past ten years we have seen the unexpected decline and fall of many famous companies whose directors believed they could go on doing business in the way they had always done it. A message now being heard loud and clear at top management meetings all over the world is that every company has to become a 'learning organisation' – which means learning much faster and in a much more radical way than ever before. Yet many managers have yet to realise that this accelerated learning process has to reach into every part of their company's operations.

Some lessons can be forced upon companies by introducing new legal offences with tougher penalties. But the crime-and-punishment solution will succeed only if it helps to make directors and managers aware that their personal responsibilities are now much wider than they were told at the start of their careers. Those responsibilities do not put a brake on commercial success but provide a means of sustaining that success through a period of social, technological and economic upheaval. If this book makes that message a little clearer it will have helped to salvage something worthwhile from the needless deaths of 192 people, most of them young, at Zeebrugge on 6 March 1987.

References

1. *Harvard Business Review*, September–October 1989.
2. *The Times*, 24 February 1990.
3. *The Times*, 28 February 1990.
4. *Ethics and Fashion in Design*, RINA, 1989.
5. *The Times*, 2 June 1987.
6. *The Daily Telegraph*, 6 April 1987.
7. *The Daily Telegraph*, 9 April 1987.

INDEX